Powerful Peace

Advance praise for J. Robert DuBois and

POWERFUL PEACE

Who else but a warrior could write so elegantly about peace? DuBois has written a potent testament to the power of peacemaking in shaping a better world. This book should be required reading for anyone interested in learning more about how to deal with the conflicts plaguing our world.

—**Reza Aslan**, author of *No god but God* and *Beyond Fundamentalism*

Powerful Peace is simple and well-written, and it's very, very interesting to read this Navy SEAL's stories from all over the world and watch him turn them around to show us ourselves. He makes you cry, he makes you laugh, and he makes you keep turning pages until it's all gone and you still want more. Read this book…and give it to people you care about.

—**Roseanne Barr**, comedic actress and
presidential candidate for the Green Tea Party

Rob DuBois writes clearly and well about how to set conditions for a world with less conflict, drawing on his rich experiences as a US Navy SEAL who has served in many countries worldwide. *Powerful Peace* is a powerful book.

—**Peter Bergen**, author of *The Longest War:
The Enduring Conflict Between America and Al-Qaeda*

In my years in the security and defense industry, I've yet to come across a book like *Powerful Peace* that inspires battle-hardened warriors and average citizens alike to join hands and uncover the sheer power of peace. In this well-written account, DuBois offers alternative concepts that refute and destabilize the popular notion of self-preservation first. With our founding fathers' brand of "we the people," he plants a seed of hope for global peace and inspires us all to imagine a world where a spirit of inclusiveness over exclusiveness spreads far and wide.

—**Eric Brown**, President, The Homeland Security Foundation of America

Powerful Peace takes you outside the everyday battle and into the hearts and minds of individuals on both sides of the culture divide; those who face ongoing struggles day to day, week to week, time after time…and how such a life changes them.

—Master Chief (Retired) **Dennis Chalker**, Plankowner of
SEAL Team SIX and Red Cell; author of *One Perfect Op:
an Insider's Account of the Navy SEAL Special Warfare Teams*

DuBois teaches us that we all have a choice when presented with adversity: powerful violence or powerful peace. Peaceful actions demonstrate to our otherwise violent neighbors here on earth that they have a choice as well. Written with the forcefulness of a soldier, yet portrayed with the heart of a deep soul, *Powerful Peace* is a must read.

—**Rob Cipriano**, President and CEO, The AllHumanity Group

When I was reading *Powerful Peace* I felt like I was hearing the Dalai Lama, crossed with a badass Navy SEAL, and with a little Monty Python mixed in.

—**Cynthia Cone**, producer of RadioIO's
Dangerous Conversation "2100 Hours" segment

For all the rhetoric in our politics about achieving peace, DuBois presents a roadmap to get us there. A man with years on the front lines of war has found yet another way to serve his country.

—**Khurram Dara**, author of *The Crescent Directive*

I first met Rob through his beautiful wife, after she and I met in a fitness club Jacuzzi. I am a blessed Muslim who enjoys the finer things in life, while following the Quran and the Sunnah of Prophet Mohamed SWA, so I was covered appropriately. That difference let Cindy and me first get to know, and then to respect one another. Peace is a powerful, religious word and any human being who pursues life with a mission to empower, educate, and bring awareness of the reality of peace is definitely a man of God. Rob is a blessing to our community and the world at large. His book should be a "must read" for any organization really searching for peace.

—**Munira A. El-Bearny**, Executive Director/Founder,
IMANI Multicultural Center

With *Powerful Peace*, Rob DuBois has created an instant game-changer in international affairs and interpersonal relationships. The book is chock full of introspective musings, interspersed with real life experiences and lessons that the author has gained, often at great cost, from his career as a Navy special operator. Those who take DuBois' lessons to heart will find the prospect of a more peaceful life and world to be more tangible than they had ever previously imagined.

—**Jeff Emanuel**, contributor to <u>RedState.com</u>
and Air Force special operations veteran

"I don't denounce violence; I embrace it." That isn't the kind of statement one would expect in a book outlining lessons on peace; but neither is this book typical of the genre. We live in remarkable times, with unprecedented challenges and entire societies that appear to be fraying at the edges. DuBois's gripping and eminently readable book *Powerful Peace* offers powerful lessons, as well as an incisive methodology for thinking about the important—and often paradoxical—work of peace-building in the twenty-first century.

—**Daveed Gartenstein-Ross**, terrorism analyst
and author of *Bin Laden's Legacy*

I have taken to heart the advice I once received not to take dietary advice from fat people or investment advice from poor people, and I do not seek advice on warfare and combat from men who have experienced neither. Rob DuBois has earned the credibility to be heard on the subject of war. Douglas MacArthur said, "The soldier, above all other people, prays for peace, for he must suffer and bear the deepest wounds and scars of war." It is in this vein that DuBois presents us with *Powerful Peace*. Those who do not know better might be surprised to see a special operations man offer a treatise on the prevention of war. I am not. Much can be learned from DuBois' writing about the prevention of bloodshed through appreciation of what we have in common.

—**Chris Graham**, Editor, The Counter Terrorist magazine

Official Washington should pay great attention to Mr. DuBois for his insight and solutions. Every American should listen to Mr. DuBois for his sense of reality and his courage of compassion. He can be a role model for both Washington and Americans. Let neither allow this man to go unheard.

—**Rob Grogan**, Editor, Front Porch Magazine

Rob DuBois has written an important book. Rob doesn't just share his experiences, although by themselves those experiences are illuminating and enlightening. Rather, he uses his own personal history to show how, as both individuals and a society, we can be stronger AND more just. Lots of people in Washington DC and the national security community talk about "smart power," but Rob takes the nearly unprecedented step of showing us how to actually apply and utilize that concept. Read this book and help create better communities and a better America.

—**Matthew Hoh**, Senior Fellow, Center for International Policy

Rob DuBois combines combat experience with a powerful sense of shared meaning and purpose. When an elite warrior speaks of Peace, there is much for us to learn; DuBois is an excellent teacher.

—**Ken Jones**, PhD, author of *When Our Troops Come Home*

From a lifetime at the tip of the sword, Rob shows that real power is beyond the hilt and in the handle. *Powerful Peace* demonstrates the concomitant relationship between War and Peace in the tip, blade and handle of the sword. Peace resides in each of us and in how we manage it, one person at a time.

—**Eric Konohia**, President, BPI Security and BPI Group

Folks in Washington know Rob DuBois, "The Velvet Glove." Now you can know the iron fist inside that glove.

—**Rear Admiral Brian Losey**, Commander,
Special Operations Command Africa

Everyone tells you what to do and what's good for you. They don't want you to find your own answers; they want you to believe in theirs. But every once in a while a book comes along that gives you the answers by helping you find them within yourself. DuBois's *Powerful Peace* is such a book. In essence it will help teach you to stop gathering information from outside yourself and start gathering it from the inside. The path of *Powerful Peace* is not in giving up what one loves, but in loving what one does. The warrior is not about winning or losing. It is not about perfection or invulnerability. It is about absolute vulnerability! This is truth. This is courage. This is *Powerful Peace*.

—**George R. Parulski, Jr.**, *Shihan* (Chief Instructor),
Okazaki-ha Shin Tenshin Shin'yo-ryu (Aiki-jujutsu), Yama-ji Kan Dojo

In *Powerful Peace*, Rob DuBois takes the reader into a very important space: the moment between action and reaction: the moment to choose your response. *Powerful Peace* is powerful, timely and thought provoking. Rob challenges preconceived notions of war and peace and those who argue they are mutually exclusive. They are not.

—**Jessica Scott**, author of *Because of You*

Powerful Peace challenges us to think differently about what defines power. Power and force are different, as only this battle tested Navy SEAL can explain.

—**Frances Townsend**, CNN National Security Contributor and former Homeland and Counterterrorism Security advisor to President Bush

Amid the chest-thumping and revelry, warriors and wanna-be's alike have missed an important message since the events of September 11th. Author Robert DuBois' Powerful Peace is precisely that message: an inspirational breakthrough in understanding the application of power from the perspective of an elite warrior. This moving, semi-autobiographical work should be required reading in disciplines ranging from diplomacy to the profession of arms, and at levels ranging from novices to seasoned veterans of war.

—**Marc Anthony Viola**, military veteran,
intelligence professional, and author of *A Spy's Résumé*

Powerful Peace sends a message that warriors and war makers need to pause and hear. It advocates a balance between smart bombs and smarter people. As a Vietnam veteran and former FBI hostage negotiator, I've seen personal conflicts evolve into bloody battles and horrific crime scenes that could have had bloodless endings if we had only practiced the principles advocated in *Powerful Peace*. This book is a message for the nations that needs to be read and practiced, one person at a time. The world has amassed the ability to kill itself; can it learn to live with itself? The answers are here in Rob's book, offered by someone who has truly been there and done that.

—**Clint Van Zandt**, former US Army Intelligence Agent, FBI Chief Hostage Negotiator, Criminal Profiler, NBC TV Senior Criminal Analyst and author of *Facing down Evil*

Your efforts to apply lessons learned to U.S. foreign policy and national security policy through "balanced peacemaking" are admirable. The experiences you and your fellow SEALs had while defending our nation and her citizens around the globe are invaluable...I commend you for reflecting on those experiences to offer key stakeholders and policymakers recommendations for securing a powerful peace.

—**Robert J. Wittman**, Member of Congress

Rob DuBois has taken a lifetime of broad experience and distilled it into lessons that can benefit us all.

—**Michael Yon**, author of *Danger Close, Moment of Truth in Iraq*, and *Iraq: Inside the Inferno, 2005-2008*

In every true warrior's epistemology, he strives for something to give him an edge on the battlefield. DuBois' conception of the fields of insight reads like a familiar mixture of Eastern and Western philosophies wrapped up in a new theoretical package. *Powerful Peace* is a true inspirational manuscript for any warrior in his quest for sharpening his most vital weapon; his mind.

—**Scott A. Zastrow**, author of *The Deguello*

With *Powerful Peace*, author J. Robert DuBois has done something more than write a book—he has committed an act of courage of the first order. Not since George Kennan, writing the article "The Sources of Soviet Conduct" under the "X" pseudonym, has there been such an articulate, well-reasoned, challenging, and inspiring call to arms. The difference is that where Kennan only gave voice to a policy, DuBois has gone a giant step further and put a human face on it. *Powerful Peace* cogently identifies the problems in today's crisis locations, challenges the mindsets that nurture them, and presents reasoned solutions. Crucially, those solutions offer hands-on capability to people of all walks of life, from minimum-wage workers to government leaders. *Powerful Peace* is not just a book; it is a tool for a better future for mankind.

—**Dwight Jon Zimmerman**, award-winning co-author of
*UNCOMMON VALOR: The Medal of Honor and
the Warriors Who Earned It in Afghanistan and Iraq*

"Life is about distinctions—a single distinction can create a profound impact and ultimately transform how we see the world around us. Go on a journey, through a Navy SEAL's eyes, as he embraces the greatest distinctions between necessary evils, truths, peace, and the power of human nature. Instead of blame he places the responsibility of peace in everyone's hands through the responsibility of individual choices. Powerful Peace is a must read for all, but especially those who wish to influence others—"It's in our decisions that destiny is shaped."

—**Tony Robbins**, Peak Performance Strategist

POWERFUL PEACE

*A Navy SEAL's
Lessons on Peace
from a
Lifetime at War*

J. ROBERT DUBOIS

NEW YORK

POWERFUL PEACE
A Navy SEAL's Lessons on Peace from a Lifetime at War

ISBN 978-1-61448-188-1 paperback
ISBN 978-1-61448-189-8 eBook
Library of Congress Control Number: 2011945351

Morgan James Publishing
The Entrepreneurial Publisher
5 Penn Plaza, 23rd Floor,
New York City, New York 10001
(212) 655-5470 office • (516) 908-4496 fax
www.MorganJamesPublishing.com

Cover Design by:
Rachel Lopez
www.r2cdesign.com

Interior Design by:
Bonnie Bushman
bonnie@caboodlegraphics.com

For my giant of a father, who has taught me that a powerful man can be gentle; and for my grandfathers, who have taught me that the greatest powers are laughter and kindness.

In memory of my friends Mike Murphy, Dan Healy and James Suh, who fell during Operation Redwing and whose sacrifices are captured by *our* friend, Marcus Luttrell, in *Lone Survivor*. Your spirits live on. By your example we will continue to fight when it's right.

TABLE OF CONTENTS

Think like a man of action, act like a man of thought.
—*Henri Bergson*

PREFACE

Cultural shift

An ounce of prevention is worth a pound of cure
—Ben Franklin

When I began my U.S. Navy career in the mid-1980s, female service members competed in striptease contests at the base club on Saturday nights. Male service members in the audience howled, stomped and shouted obscenities at their "equal partners" up on stage.

On Monday mornings, we all suited up and worked side-by-side in our government offices. Back in the workplace, a man who had openly leered at a woman's most intimate areas was prohibited from voicing rude observations about her figure. Sexual harassment was against military law. On Saturday nights, however, it was a social imperative.

Is this hypocritical disconnect incomprehensible today? If so, that's because a deep cultural shift has made it so. Today's military culture remains necessarily rougher than that of the civilian sector, yet it's light years ahead

---

There simply are not as many *intractable*
or *inevitable* conflicts between cultures and
groups as we may have been taught.

---

of those earlier days when we would compartmentalize periodic degradation away from the mandated "equality" of duty hours.

Conflict, whether interpersonal or international, is ripe for a similar cultural shift in understanding, educating and behavior. Some of the assumptions we've grown up with are flawed. There simply are not as many *intractable* or *inevitable* conflicts between cultures and groups as we may have been taught. Such hardened beliefs on conflict—much like the obsolete military dichotomy between office behavior and social misbehavior—are the legacy of once-useful protectionist thinking.

Us-and-Them thinking served an important purpose when primitive tribes barely survived on scarce resources, and the appearance of a stranger presented a likely challenge to that survival. Unfortunately, as mankind's capacity to produce necessities and offset scarcity has increased, our underlying tendency for suspicion has not diminished. We are still captives of "zero-sum" thinking—one side must lose for the other to win—and not looking hard enough at the magnifying power of sober cooperation. Worse, the fear of Others can become a self-fulfilling prophecy. Some of my most dangerous colleagues share my frustration that military operations do not yet adequately address the needs of local national civilians in preventing further causes for conflict.

On the other hand, force is still sometimes the most appropriate course, whether during paralyzed negotiations or in specific threat circumstances. I'll prove that to you shortly. Enraged or deranged individuals do sometimes present an immediate danger to innocents, children included. Groups can send fanatical suicide bombers to kill indiscriminately. In that terrible moment, violence is often the *only* course to prevent annihilation. I invite my pacifist friends to skip ahead to chapter four to read about my Marine commando friend Sean and his split-second choice for force—violence—that saved dozens of lives.

This dual reality, or duality, on the use of force is the bedrock for our concept of "balanced peacemaking."

I would also invite my proud and/or arrogant friends (pacifist, belligerent or in-between) to skip ahead to chapters twenty and twenty-one, titled "Pride" and "Arrogance" respectively. As you'll read in the Introduction, these themes repeat throughout the book alongside Transparency, Sacrifice, Humanity and other essential ingredients of balanced peacemaking. Forgive me in advance; Powerful Peace will challenge every reader at some point along the way, but take comfort that only you will know which areas sting most. By way of example I'll admit: I am convicted that

Humility is absolutely necessary in cutting away roots of conflict, yet even in my own life its maintenance is a daily struggle.

History is replete with examples of thinking that has outlived its usefulness. In earlier days it was acceptable to buy and sell human beings as property, with all the rights of ownership that reduced humans to thinking, feeling livestock. (In parts of the world today, as you will read, this practice continues…and there is something you can do about it.) In various places and times this has included the right to end a slave's life on a whim.

Yes, some of what seems deeply repugnant today was once commonplace. In the first half of the 20th century in some parts of the United States, a dominant race of men freely beat, framed for crimes and even hanged members of a less empowered group of American citizens. And as described, during the latter half of that century, we rewarded public degradation of active duty women in the military services.

What about tomorrow's "today?" Some of what we think and do right now will seem similarly out of place, in retrospect. Yet as the clock ticks toward the next conflict, we no longer have the luxury of waiting for glacial societal change to update our thinking. The few, whether defenders or hostile actors, can now impact the many as never before in history. Those who protect have to act with greater urgency. The good news is that through improved understanding, we can make conflict prevention a sort of second nature. Our choices today affect many tomorrows; not only for friends and enemies but for total strangers on the other side of this increasingly interconnected world.

We must adapt. Just during the year it took to write Powerful Peace, the human race crossed the historic threshold of *seven billion* members. If unprecedented technological advances are allowed to run ahead of rational, compassionate, and moral human guidance, the consequences will be devastating. We have become like antagonistic passengers on a planet-sized vessel; like it or not, we need to work together to stay afloat. This all begins with an examination of assumptions about our shipmates, our ship and our seas. And it gives us the insight to pick the best course.

If unprecedented technological advances are allowed to run ahead of rational, compassionate, and moral human guidance, the consequences will be devastating.

A personal letter to veterans and recruits

Before we get into a book about making peace for your neighborhood and your nation, I want to take a moment to speak to a very special class of people in every land. Those who have served, do serve and will serve the rest of us deserve to be acknowledged specially in any discussion of war and peace. Following years of complex, sometimes-ambiguous, violent conflicts around the globe, many have been wounded in obvious and not-so-obvious ways.

Ours is a noble calling: the honor and privilege of ensuring the safety of others. Try not to doubt that, whether you have seen, or will see, events that trouble you during your service. I'm proud of you, and I beg every protected citizen to stand up and humbly thank you.

Your body, your mind, your heart and your soul have been scarred, or will be scarred, by your transformation into a warrior. This is the price of duty. It has built, or will build, your character and strength.

You may be in pain, struggling with a lost limb, lost peace of mind…or a lost friend. Talk about it. Talk about it. Find the courage to trust someone else, perhaps a professional, and talk about it. Believe me; I know how scary it can be to open up. Express your fears of weakness in a trusted relationship. It *will* make you stronger.

Yes, big boys and big girls do cry. It's only the incomplete woman, the frightened man, who cannot release that most basic human expression. Whether a pilot, a grunt, a SEAL or a cook, there is no place for robots in our business. It's only through teamwork that you have become, or will become, a soldier. And it's only through teamwork that you honor your comrades and live up to your full potential. I pray your life will be deeply fulfilled, and your healing complete.

For 24/7 veterans' crisis support, or to just begin opening up, call **1-800-273-TALK**.

> **Out of suffering have emerged the strongest souls;**
> **the most massive characters are seared with scars.**
> —*Khalil Gibran*

AUTHOR'S NOTE

Powerful Peace **is a** shot across the bow of the ignorance and misunderstanding that underlie conflict. No culture, creed or color on earth *desires* to live in fear or insecurity, and yet none of us takes full advantage of the peacemaking potential in deeper understanding. Because solutions are discovered through sharing, we've established a global forum for sharing at PeaceHawks.org. Here you can read about people and organizations already making a difference, and you can make a difference of your own by sharing personal stories of overcoming conflict and finding hope. Please join us. The only cost to become a Peace Hawk is a willingness to care. Lend your voice and hands today to the peace, happiness and security of our children's future children.

Write with me
Please don't open Powerful Peace without a pen close at hand. This book is full of ideas and I want you to scribble in your own—that's what margins are for. Bend the pages; underline the bits you love or hate; engage! I want to hear from you, too. Since this is the beginning of a global dialogue, let's talk. You can reach me at Robert@PowerfulPeace.NET, or connect with me at Twitter.com as *RobDuBois*.

Starting sharing
Five percent of author's royalties will be donated to Save the Children to improve the lives of kids, and thus improve our shared future. Save the Children programs are dedicated to protection, health, nutrition, and education for kids across the globe... including those in need in my own United States.

ACKNOWLEDGMENTS

People in my field are usually too focused on defending against threats to address their prevention. Yet Powerful Peace has come about anyway, and it exists only through the immeasurable contribution of those family and friends…and of those enemies…who are its ultimate authors.

Shelves today are filled with books by and about U.S. Navy SEALs. That may have attracted your attention in this case, but Powerful Peace is different. It isn't about my being a SEAL so much as the privilege that has given me to see the amazing things you'll read, and to know amazing people. Marcus Luttrell wrote *Lone Survivor* to remember men who are admired across much of the world for their tremendous ability and sacrifice under fire. Whether these heroes earned Medals of Honor, or you've never heard of them, they are to us simply friends who are deeply missed and called Dan, and Mike, and James, and more…. Many of my friends still serving cannot be identified, of course, but I'll whisper some first names to honor the selflessness and courage of Rik, and Christian, and Roger, and Brian, and Saint, and Jimbo, and the Shauns….

If not for my agent, Michael Ebeling, who envisioned the potential of an unconventional project nobody else would pick up, this book would not exist. I'm eternally grateful for your insight and experience, Michael. Equally daring would have to be David Hancock and his incredible staff at Morgan James Publishing, Lyza Poulin, Bethany Marshall and Rachel Lopez, who caught this vision and threw their remarkable talent and passion behind our shared dream of balanced peacemaking.

Rounding out the book team is editor Rob Grogan, whose Front Porch Magazine first gave me the opportunity to produce a column—which led to a blog—which led to national articles—which led to Powerful Peace. He stepped up and molded this draft manuscript into a book worth reading. "Peer editors" of note, who helped this project from its extremely rocky start, include good friends Matthew Hoh, Ben Nerud, Matt Nelson, Bill Nigh and Marc Viola, author of *A Spy's Resume*.

Friends around the world have lived out the following lessons, whether heartbreakingly bloody or heartwarmingly promising. I've observed, processed and recorded them in the hope we might spare one child, one day, from terrible suffering—of losing a parent, a limb or her life—to grow up happy, healthy and old...and touch who-knows-how-many more lives. You, my friends, are Hayri, and Jamal, and Kevin, and Roman, and Talib, and Alex, and Burhan, and Jerry, and Kamy, and Stefan, and Rashid, and Munira, and the rest whose names would fill these pages and leave no room for your stories. I am enriched because you have shared the gift of your lives. To those I have not captured here, my apologies—and my deepest gratitude for your undeserved gift.

My grandparents, parents, sisters and teachers laid the keel and set the course for the life I sailed out into this wide world. I will never be as fine a grandson, son, brother or student as you deserve, but I promise to keep trying.

There is a "last" in every list. They are often a "last-but-not-least." That has never been truer than in the case of my little family. They have endured many *years* without me during duty overseas, and thousands of hours more while I write on our front porch or at our local Starbucks. My sons Gabe and Jack are my greatest pride. Their future service to our species will make my brief time on earth seem like an unproductive flicker. My daughter Effie is my greatest joy. Her future art will illuminate the world with love and peace. And my wife...my wife. Cindy, everything I have that is good in this life has come through you. Thank you. ILU.

INTRODUCTION
Surreal...and so real

The death of Osama bin Laden at the hands of my fellow SEALs closed a transformative, decade-long chapter of my own life. As you'll read, my deployed platoon was actively involved in the "Global War on Terror" from the very first minutes of the September 11th attacks. Ten years later, other SEALs closed the book on bin Laden's hate-filled existence.

We have reached the time for the world to look for, and work for, a better and safer and brighter future together. This future demands new thinking; the vicious cycle of escalating violence is not inevitable, but it can seem to be the default setting for our species. The stakes are rising and we need to get much, much smarter to rewrite our self-destructive second nature and pre-empt the next bin Laden.

His life was marked by a cancerous hatred which ultimately left him hiding, isolated in a physical and emotional prison of his own making. Through the persistent

---

The stakes are rising and we need to get much,
much smarter to rewrite our self-destructive second
nature and pre-empt the next bin Laden.

---

corrosion of his choices, he ultimately rendered himself unable to stroll outside the fortress that became his home, unable to run downtown on a simple errand, and unable even to chat with his neighbors in a carefree, life-giving moment of human connection. Such years of non-life should serve as a valuable lesson to those of us who still draw breath and desire lives worth living. *Choices matter.*

Our viewpoint is informed by our experiences, and our experiences are created in part by our decisions—decisions about where to be, what to learn, and with whom to spend time. Bin Laden was committed to being the self-appointed judge, jury and executioner of strangers worldwide. Although the scale of his destruction was rare in its excess, it reflects a common pattern of human conflict—he became fixed on the righteousness of his beliefs to a tragically absurd extreme that harmed innocents.

His obsession cost the lives of thousands, caused the suffering of hundreds of thousands, fostered animosity and violence toward millions of *those he claimed to defend*, and irrevocably paved the road to his own final moment—and a bullet in the face.

This larger-than-life founder of a murderous movement finished his days as a washed-up old man hunched in stocking cap and blanket, locked away and peering wistfully at news clips of himself from more significant—more relevant—days.

I feel no pity for the terrorist who died in that compound in Pakistan, but I'm heartbroken for the child he once was…and the man he could have been. In the beginning, even Osama bin Laden was an innocent infant. Through a series of external events and internal decisions he became the monster we remember. Ridiculous and tragic wars between global powers rise and fall on the same variables. At some point along the way he didn't have to become the "Osama bin Laden" of future history books. With the vast resources he was born to inherit, he could have improved many lives rather than destroy.

Also, and without apology for the unimaginable pain inflicted by this mass murderer, he and his followers did not carry out the attacks of 9/11 in a social or psychological vacuum. You will read about legitimate grievances which have been hijacked for grossly illegitimate purposes.

You will read about legitimate grievances which have been hijacked for grossly illegitimate purposes.

The universal principle of balancing courage
with compassion applies in the boardroom,
in the bedroom, and on the battlefield.

I'm no stranger to conflict, hate and violence, as you will read in Powerful Peace. And you may be surprised to accept that in "balanced peacemaking" there are occasions for necessary violence. But this isn't about me. It's not about bin Laden. It's about *all* of us. In stories from our lifetimes at war you can read stories of yourself and your loved ones. We all have a great deal in common, and that's the key to balanced peacemaking. In fact, I'll ask you to express more of your own story as we go along, through our network at PeaceHawks.org and in your ongoing personal commitment to make peace wherever you stand. You might even help write future books on Powerful Peace, which is really just the first of many stories in making the world a little safer for all.

Here you'll read about men, women, and children who have suffered, and who will suffer. You'll read about interpersonal and international conflict, its origins, and some important alternatives to repeating the same, sad mistakes. Wherever you find yourself on the use-of-force continuum, you'll understand that force is sometimes essential. Try to imagine your limited options if a suicide bomber were to approach your family, or a vicious man were brutalizing your small child. Immediate action—force if available—would not only be appropriate, but necessary. Necessary violence has its place. Yet the use of force without discretion, without a sort of "ruthless restraint," sows seeds that yield unintended, undesirable, and painful future situations for our loved ones and ourselves. The universal principle of balancing courage with compassion applies in the boardroom, in the bedroom, and on the battlefield.

In service to innocent victims of conflict worldwide, I'll shamelessly drop names of friends of Powerful Peace from the military, government, academia and the private sector. You'll recognize some from today's headlines. This cornucopia of talent demonstrates that there need not be any limits to our efforts to ensure security. Solutions spring from creative thinking, and humanity's imagination is unlimited. Look at what Steve Jobs did to the universe of computing with just silicon and an insistence that it be simpler. Can we not do the same and more with the universal raw materials of heart and mind?

...you'll recognize the reactive and sometimes unnecessary roots of hate, and understand that those roots strangle all involved.

This book is for young men and women stepping out into the world; for good people interested in helping their neighborhoods; for the yet-untested and the veterans of war and other foreign service; and for leaders of armies and governments across the globe...perhaps especially for this last group. It is for believers from any faith, and for those who believe in none. It is also for citizens of nations about whom much is assumed, but little is understood; and for nations, like the United States, to whom much has been given and from whom much is justifiably expected. This book is intended to offer a voice to all, to open a dialogue for clarity that can contribute to peace and teach us the lessons of balanced peacemaking. We can no longer disregard balance with so much on the line.

We can choose fearless and civil discourse at this critical juncture in history. The alternative is to sit by while technological strides and ideological divides rip the world apart.

In these pages you'll witness the tragic and absurd losses from conflict in the bloody, muddy sand of war and in generations of wounding wrought by chronic social feuds. You'll increase your capacity and desire to undermine conflict. You'll focus on real, tangible, attainable peace. And you'll recognize the reactive and sometimes unnecessary roots of hate, and understand that those roots strangle all involved.

A brief example: during my early Navy years a friend once walked through a crowded bar carrying a full pitcher of beer in each hand. Partway back to the table, a young woman spun to face him and loudly accused him of having groped her. Looking left and right between his firmly-held pitchers, he was even more amazed to be confronted by her angry boyfriend asking, "Did you grab her butt?" My impatient, imprudent and somewhat inebriated shipmate then did the only thing that made sense to him in the moment. He hit the boyfriend in the face with a pitcher of beer.

Each participant in this spectacle disregarded the obvious. The girlfriend could have noticed two full pitchers and the impossibility of groping. The boyfriend, likewise. My friend could have thought of the potentially tragic consequences of shattering a glass pitcher in a man's face (which, fortunately, didn't happen—he was drenched in beer, but not in blood). Each could have, but instead chose this Dance of Fools—a dance of compounding deficits of good judgment. The price that accompanies this dance among national powers is significantly higher.

Because of pride and fear, it is difficult to admit—or even recognize—one's role in the Dance of Fools. Every error and subsequent rationalization of wrong behavior squeezes a participant ever more tightly into a defensive posture. This dynamic renders us nearly incapable of accomplishing that simplest of steps for conflict resolution: Just Stop Fighting…I call it "Cause a Pause," or CAP. This is similar to that delightful expression used in gang warfare, "bust a cap." Between rival gangs in the United States, this is a euphemism for shooting somebody. In the realm of peacemaking, I urge that we learn to "bust a CAP" to undermine conflict *before* anybody needs to get shot.

Between armed groups, or in a war of words between lovers, there can be no solution before the striking stops. Pause. More often than not, mistakes and assumptions represent a greater enemy than the human opposing us. This is why I highlight the role of misunderstanding as the insidious root of so much conflict.

I have many enemies, but few that walk and talk. Instead of "Ivan" and "Omar," they have names like Rape as a weapon of war; Abuse of innocent children; Mistrust among cultures…Hatreds founded on misunderstanding.

Every side can agree on the worst of all losses: the broken or crippled bodies or hearts of the youngest among us, caught in the crossfire of hate in action. Fighting carries many other costs as well, both obvious and hidden. What about the incredible price of defending against *imagined* threats?

Each of us can make a difference if we first accept some uncomfortable truths. We can begin by examining our own worldviews and our impact on others. Anything less is theoretical playtime. We also have to examine the news and views that are set before us. The true stories and examples in Powerful Peace will help you develop a greater capacity to see into and disrupt the heart of hate. Disentangling conflict begins with the self.

The true stories and examples in Powerful Peace will help you develop a greater capacity to see into and disrupt the heart of hate.

The book is divided into four sections, named after the four elements of balanced human life: Body, Mind, Heart and Soul. We are more than just walking lumps of animal instinct. This balanced arrangement corresponds with the "rational, compassionate and moral human guidance" previously described, seeking a broader understanding of our common ground. Ideas progress through the book's evolving chapters, laying out critical themes like Humility, Dignity, Respect, Courage and Accountability. Because we share one world, I'll pull references from across the planet and across society.

As the late, greatly irreverent George Carlin so eloquently demonstrated, reality is a very funny place. Popular culture on TV and film reflects our complex existence in tidy 30- or 90-minute bites with just the right amounts of drama, romance, and humor. So I'll begin this cultural exploration by urging you to watch the movie *Crash* (Lion's Gate, 2004), which is both superbly illustrative of tragic human destruction and superbly titled for our subject. The story involves families, from very different cultures, crashing together on the stage of daily life around Los Angeles. True to life, there are startlingly unexpected and unnecessary turns in its violent course. One of the stars of *Crash* is Don Cheadle, who played the lead in a true story of genocide in *Hotel Rwanda* (MGM/United Artists, 2004). That role educated him on the catastrophe of ethnic cleansing in Africa and, as you will read, motivated him to take an active role in preventing genocide and other forms of violence.

Besides the hidden or apparent wisdom in these books and films, I'll give you some of my favorite quotes from others; sometimes profound, sometimes coarse, always edifying. Please give each a moment's thought.

As we journey together, we'll encounter some true-to-life "elephants in the room" that nobody wants to talk about. I'll walk you straight up to examine those elephants. Like a little boy in a fable, I'll raise my voice and point directly at the emperor with no clothes. His foolishness is no longer a simple embarrassment; now it costs the lives and limbs of children.

I'll raise my voice and point directly at the emperor with no clothes. His foolishness is no longer a simple embarrassment; now it costs the lives and limbs of children.

Powerful Peace is not so much a one-time
prescription as it is preventive medicine;
a way of looking at the world.

During years of advising military commanders and policy makers, I've observed unrealized potential for peacemaking. We live in a generation of unprecedented openness between societies and groups, with equally unprecedented accessibility to information. We have the opportunity to establish an entirely new understanding of differences, disputes, defenses and destructive powers. Heads of state and schoolteachers can dialogue via Twitter with hardened opponents and champions of *jihad*. We have the opportunity to learn about others, from others. And we have the opportunity to harness the incredible talent and critical thinking of a great generation of future global leaders; we need only reach out and begin.

Powerful Peace is not so much a one-time prescription as it is preventive medicine; a way of looking at the world. It represents a conversational path toward transformation. The time has come to change our minds—our way of thinking—across the planet, and to un-think much of what we currently take for granted; things like who hates who, why, and the supposed inevitability of destructive conflict. Our future is not yet written. Daily, we are scratching out and doodling in our very best efforts to script a future and dismantle outdated systems that today cause more insecurity than they prevent.

I hope you won't agree with everything in this book. If you did, I'd worry that one of us is trying too hard to please the other. But I have confidence much of it will ring true for you as it has for thousands of others...and for thousands of years. I've invented nothing. The Golden Rule and concepts of consequences are not new material in the scope of human history. This may just be the latest reminder of some things we've forgotten about ourselves.

In the end, I'll ask that you not keep this book. I'll ask you to give it away—perhaps to a young person just setting out to make a mark in the world, or to your neighbor, or to a soldier trying to make sense of his painful experiences...perhaps to your senator at her next public event. And I'll ask international readers to take this opportunity to make themselves heard in a global forum we build together at PeaceHawks.org. I'll ask you to share these ideas, so my own children can be safer when we all grow up.

I'll ask you to share these ideas, so my own children can be safer when we all grow up.

In any case, I hope this process of humanization will increase you. I wish you peace. A balanced, powerful peace.

SECTION I

BODY

The Physical

Food before fun

Abraham Maslow taught that if a person lacks satisfaction of basic survival needs, she will be incapable of working at a higher, cooperative level, even if it's in her own best interests. It is difficult to be gracious when starving, or hurting. Cyclical and escalating conflict over meager resources is one by-product of desperation. Since lashing out produces further hurt and increased desperation, the cycle is very difficult to break—as we are witnessing around the world.

An empty belly has no ears.
—*Proverb attributed to China, Haiti, Senegal et al*

1　HATE
September 11, 2001

The history of violent conflict traces back in many oral traditions to the very first humans. This opening chapter offers a first-hand account of one of the most hate-based and hate-producing events of modern history. Close the book for a moment, and take a second look at the cover. The number in the bottom-right corner of my photo is the original date stamp of that shot, taken while training Arab SEALs at their base in the Middle East. It was exactly seven days before September 11, 2001. And it was exactly seven days after my wife and children flew out of Boston on a flight number that two weeks later would be incinerated and immortalized in fire and blood. Yes, friends…I am familiar with hate.

In hatred as in love, we grow like the thing we brood upon.
What we loathe, we graft into our very soul.
— *Mary Renault*

My American SEAL platoon and our Arab SEAL hosts watched in living color on satellite television as the second plane dissolved into the second of the Twin Towers. It was approaching evening where we were, several months into a deployment to the Persian Gulf. We sat frozen, burning in silent rage, staring as nearly twenty deluded murderers exploited the most advanced technology to carry out the most primitive evil. Having slashed women to death with razor knives, these "men" committed

Teammate Shaun Marriott and I perfect the art of force application. (Note brass shell ejecting above scope.)

suicide, proving they were brave enough and strong enough to kill thousands of innocents—among them unsuspecting office workers, little old ladies, and infants.

These murderers called themselves "warriors."

We were all naval commandos in that room, some American, others the "local nationals" we had been sent to train. Ironically painful and poignant, we had been teaching our hosts skills that would make them better at killing terrorists. Yet not one of us could lift a finger to prevent what was happening in the United States.

As we sat together in that remote Middle Eastern barracks, each was very much alone with his thoughts. The Americans thought of loved ones and Teammates a world away. My Arab friends thought of...well, I hope to one day share another cup of tea and ask them. (As you may imagine, things got a little busy during the days that followed. Within weeks, I would be conducting reconnaissance for the invasion of Afghanistan.)

There we all were. Nearly twenty Arabs and Americans, living together in those barracks; nearly twenty Arabs, dying together in dispersed teams of terrorist hijackers. Had those cowardly bastards chosen to face our little international group,

---

We sat frozen, burning in silent rage, staring as nearly twenty deluded murderers exploited the most advanced technology to carry out the most primitive evil.

Had those cowardly bastards chosen to face
our little international group, man to man,
9/11 would have turned out differently.

man to man, 9/11 would have turned out differently. They wouldn't have had to work so hard to make their way to hell, for one thing. At our hands, hell would have come up roaring to greet them.

And three thousand gentle, innocent souls would still be alive with their families.

Not one word was spoken for hours during the spectacle. If one of the local SEALs had laughed or expressed any satisfaction in what we were witnessing, I believe I would have killed him on the spot. This is not a boast. It's a confession, a shameful admission. I'm very ashamed it's true. These were my friends, but we were so choked with hurt; we were so thirsty for revenge.

Here was a bitterly painful sense of helplessness, for some of the most dangerous men on earth. We were supposed to be the protectors of our countrymen. Each December Seventh at the SEAL Delivery Vehicle (SDV) Team in Hawaii, in fact, we swam the five miles around Pearl Harbor's Ford Island. Commemorating the original Day of Infamy in 1941, this ceremony sent the message that hostile actors were welcome to attack again if they wished…we would be ready this time.

Instead, in September sixty years later, we were on the wrong side of the planet.

We were supposed to be the ones who would sacrifice all so fellow citizens could sleep safe in their beds at night. Yet we would sleep through that night with troubled dreams, safe in our own beds, while thousands of innocents under our protection suffered and died in a crushing, inescapable nightmare.

In addition, within our platoon I had the unique awareness that only two Tuesdays earlier, my wife and children had flown from Boston to California, just as a plane I had watched disintegrate had been scheduled to do. Later, my wife would tell me a strange detail. During the early part of their flight on August 28th, a man of apparent Middle Eastern descent had been roaming the cabin and studying the passenger seating, crew stations, wings and more. He had been carrying an Arabic language newspaper. She wrote it off as unreasonable suspicion on her part, but remained troubled by his intense focus on surveying the airplane…especially the wings. Of course, this may have all been coincidence.

I sat among Arab friends and allies in the Middle East and watched 9/11 unfold.

It is no coincidence, however, that I have a personal understanding of hatred. That's the first thing I want you to understand.

Unlike my loved ones sobbing through a tortured morning rush hour in the United States, I sat among Arab friends and allies in the Middle East and watched 9/11 unfold. Some in my mixed group of highly trained commandos may have empathized with the grievances of the al Qaeda (AQ) terrorists piloting those improvised cruise missiles.

If that last statement strains your comfort level, I'm satisfied. Peacemaking is not the fluffy stuff of rainbows and unicorns. It is not exclusive to well-intentioned activists shouting "Ban War!" Peacemaking is the right—and the burden—of all of us, and it sometimes includes the use of force. Without just war, Hitler's quest would have destroyed millions more. Genuine conflict reduction requires the capacity and willingness to strike, combined with a determined restraint and the guts to stare straight into the face of hate…and then choose a reasoned response.

Yes, some of my friends did (and do) empathize with the grievances AQ uses to justify hijacking airplanes. Note the careful use of this phrase "*empathize with the grievances.*" I know none of our Arab partners in that host platoon were radicalized terrorists. If one had been, he would have exploited our trust and killed us while we slept. The symbolic value of slaughtering a few American SEALs would have been irresistible. As demonstrated by the 9/11 hijackers, even sacrificing his own life to accomplish this would have been acceptable to an extremist with an opportunity.

This may be difficult to reconcile according to our ordinary sense of reality, but we are in extraordinary times. Extraordinary times call for extraordinary effort. If we have the courage to consider the Other's reality, *empathy with grievances* is possible and productive.

Here's one poorly hidden elephant in the room: Unresolved grievances and the anxieties they compel keep solutions at arm's length. In many of the countries I've

---

Peacemaking is not the fluffy stuff of rainbows and unicorns.

---

visited around the Middle East, the horror of Palestinian children killed in Israeli attacks is advertised widely and discussed passionately. For Israelis, on the other hand, the constant threat of devastating Palestinian rocket and suicide bomber attacks is a deep and chronic pain that can make reasoned negotiation seem unreasonable. Neither side will ever run out of iron-clad reasons to avenge the pain it has suffered; nor will either side ever accept its own marginalization or elimination, *so all the struggle and rhetoric in pursuit of dominance for either extreme can only serve to prolong the suffering of innocents within both populations.*

Many participants can sense this. Isn't it time many more admitted it? Isn't it time both parties, with their thoughts on their children, stared straight into the face of hate and said "Enough?"

As mentioned earlier, actor/director Don Cheadle and humanitarian John Prendergast have done exactly that in another abscess of raging human conflict in another part of the world. You'll read about their "Enough Project" and book, *The Enough Moment*, in chapter 25 on Commonality.

Only the absolute cessation of violence allows space to work through underlying issues and pursue stability and reconciliation to benefit both parties.

Only the absolute cessation of violence allows space to work through underlying issues and pursue stability and reconciliation to benefit both parties. Yet all too often, hatred is so intense that a participant will choose personal suffering over personal peace as the price required to cause his adversary pain.

Until squabbling siblings, barroom brawlers or aggressing armies establish at least a cold truce, until the participants can "cause a pause," the cycle of retaliatory violence continues to escalate and solutions fly ever further from reality...and more innocents suffer for our folly. At the most basic level there is no such thing as a corporation, an army, a nation, or even the book club where you may be reading this—each of these entities is nothing more than a collection of individual human beings in willing cooperation, backed up in some cases by lists which are also nothing more than shared understandings between individuals.

The human is the lowest common denominator, from the smallest to the greatest social organization we have ever established. This universal individuality,

The solution lies not at but between the extremes. Only here can balance—and peace for those under your care—be found.

to be revisited later on in the sections on Heart and Soul, is the reason peace cannot spread except by individual choices and actions...like *yours*. Understanding and peace don't come about by some mysterious accident while we squabble over crumbs. Boardroom, bedroom and battlefield are universally populated only by individual human beings, and only those who consciously choose and act can improve conditions for all of us.

The solution lies not at but *between* the extremes. Only here can balance—and peace for those under your care—be found.

2   HARM
Blowing up baby

The cycle of hate naturally results in a desire to harm. Sometimes children and other vulnerable members of a population are deliberately targeted. More often, they are harmed (emotionally and physically) because they were in the wrong place at the right time during an attack against some "legitimate" target, ranging from an estranged spouse to an enemy soldier. There have been casualties of war for as long as there have been wars—but once we acknowledge that some fights are not worth fighting, we find ourselves accountable to prevent as many as possible.

> **Darkness cannot drive out darkness; only light can do that.**
> **Hate cannot drive out hate; only love can do that.**
> —*Martin Luther King, Jr.*

I happened upon a photo of two little girls who had been blown up by al Qaeda in Iraq (AQI) at their school in Kirkuk on April 2, 2007. It's my favorite picture; I keep it as a screen saver to remind me of who I serve and to put my own troubles in context.

I work for them and others like them. They don't pay me for my work, but those who do pay me understand that, ultimately, I work for those little girls.

They say a picture is worth a thousand words. The pain, terror and anguish of the precious children in this silent image speak deafeningly.

9

These beautiful children were seriously injured by an al Qaeda car bombing near their school. Their friends died. (Credit: Emad Matti / AP)

These small girls, probably about four and eight years of age, sit on a hospital table with their faces twisted in pain. Both are having a very bad hair day—exploding cars will do that to a person. The younger has thick, curly locks and, except for being covered in her own blood, could be a little Arab Shirley Temple.

Although most of the blood soaking her white T-shirt and pants is probably from a minor but fast-flowing scalp wound, you can just make out that her delicate right hand is damaged, too. She's favoring it to keep it from touching anything. She needs desperately to be held, and seems to be reaching for someone off camera... with little gold bracelets dripping blood, she's feeling a million miles away from the security, love and peace she so deserves. It is a peace she will never again fully know.

"Hard power" (the capacity to use violence or some other coercive force) will always be a necessary element in the real world. You'll read more about it in chapter 4. There will always be people who will not pause long enough to be reached by any other means. For them, we bring the force fulcrum all the way to the harshest end of the scale. This was the self-selected fate of Osama bin Laden. And though you will read much more in Powerful Peace about additional alternatives, sometimes violence is the only appropriate course of action. My uniformed brothers continue that mission, even as I press on with my new calling in front of a keyboard.

God, how I long to suit up and rejoin the mission! I want to pay back, to the monsters that did this, everything they deserve—with interest. If you came to this

There will always be people who will not pause long enough to be reached by any other means.

I don't denounce violence; I embrace it.

---

table for a Kumbaya solution, you'll be disappointed. I don't denounce violence; I embrace it. I keep violence as close as my hands and my heart. Because I do, I am more often spared from having to use it. My heart doesn't ache for these children. It explodes. Forcing out burning tears, my heart explodes like the car bomb that tore them and their playmates apart.

Yet despite a boiling rage, I remind myself—we must not abandon balance. We have to respond, not react. In the next chapter, we'll look more at the Why Not of lashing out, but for now let me just say: to become more effective, we have to learn to engage among and across relationships, households, and societies—most especially into concentrations where the hatred is most firmly rooted. Destroying alone leads to more destroying. This is the terrible paradox. It's almost impossible to imagine breaking the cycle of harm when you feel so hurt and hateful, but there is no other hope for these girls and millions like them.

If we don't reduce harm on the wider scale through improved interpersonal and international relations, this will happen again, and again, and again…and again.

Because I do, I am more often spared from having to use it.

---

3 LOSS
Everybody loses

The cycle of harm, by its very intention, results in loss for one or more parties. During one assignment with the U.S. Special Forces in Iraq, I attended the memorial service of a brother soldier killed in the line of duty. This loss was a somber occasion that inspired me to recall and blend stories of loss from all perspectives. The experience painted a systemic image of the interdependent, connective tissue of self-perpetuating violence which sometimes feels so natural as to seem inescapable. Courageous men and women have to reject the lethal spiral. Courageous men and women are the last hope when fires of hatred threaten to consume us all.

> **Two aged men, that had been foes for life,**
> **Met by a grave, and wept—and in those tears**
> **They washed away the memory of their strife;**
> **Then wept again the loss of all those years.**
> **—***Jean Paul*

Us

We honor a fallen comrade. Hundreds of strangers converge from all corners of our little camp in Iraq. America the Beautiful plays quietly, reverently, as members from all services, agencies, and companies walk up, one by one, filing into clean ranks.

> They know they are fortunate just to have a doctor's attention; that he lacks anesthesia is a cost of being born here.

Our chaplain takes the podium, in his uniform and matching camouflage-patterned military stole, bringing our attention to God's sovereignty over this solemn event. He speaks of a family's loss and a hero's honor.

Them

In the adjacent Iraqi town outside the base, a mother and father clutch at each other and weep desperately. They cannot know yet whether their four-year-old daughter will survive the shrapnel wounds torn deep into her abdomen, thigh, and scalp. They know they are fortunate just to have a doctor's attention; that he lacks anesthesia is a cost of being born here.

Us

Our commander steps to the microphone. He praises the selflessness of this man who had gone forward time and again into harm's way. The commander has lost many brothers, in many battles. He bears the pain with practiced stoicism. He praises the courage of a good man whose child will never again fall asleep under Daddy's comforting smile; whose wife will never again melt into those strong arms.

The man's wife and child have been notified of their devastating loss. An irreplaceable piece of their own souls died on the side of the road, with their man, on that day.

Them

The mother and father now sit numb. Their hearts died the instant the doctor failed to save their little girl. They stare vacantly through red and swollen eyes as his staff cares for the small, torn daughters of other families.

Us

Six thousand miles away in the United States, a nation snarls and chews at itself. Citizens complain that elections are only a choice for the lesser of evils. National

---

The media stoke the flames of dissatisfaction, telling pieces of truth to uphold the assumptions of their owners.

---

unity fades to a distant memory, mere flickers of the brotherhood that shone after those horrific terrorist attacks during one breakfast in the new millennium.

The media stoke the flames of dissatisfaction, telling pieces of truth to uphold the assumptions of their owners. Ratings rise. Competing outlets create divergent realities. "News" programs become thinly-veiled political support machines. Sales of advertised products soar as each camp more zealously devours its own "news." The very real enemies of freedom and democracy around the world cackle with glee at a spectacle of national disharmony driven by selfish, divisive gain.

Them

The dead girl's fourteen-year-old brother had been a gentle boy, destined for musical greatness that might have lifted the hearts of millions. Now, his own heart destroyed by hate, he vows to join the resistance against the insurgency and kill as many as possible. Within the month, he will destroy three other families' sons…before being shot to death.

Elsewhere in town, an armed group converges on a lightly-occupied mosque during prayers and takes seven worshipers away. These men are the wrong "type" of Muslim, and the subsequent brutality of their deaths will horrify and pacify the neighbors of seven abruptly fatherless families. It is possible to be tortured to death.

Seven more mothers and wives are utterly shattered. Each will suffer terribly at the loss of her husband; learning that he himself suffered terribly in a slow death will be far worse. Worst of all will be the desperate years of begging or whoring to feed hungry children.

We

My thoughts return to our ceremony beneath a blazing sun. The heat is oppressive. There is so much loss.

I ache, deeply, for my own. Before he was killed, this was my brother in this world. It is my loss that this good man is dead.

I have lost this little girl, my precious sister in this world.

I have lost the rational, respectful discourse with my countrymen that determines who will lead one great and undivided nation.

I have lost the kind and gentle boy who would heal souls with his music.

I have lost the seven husbands and fathers and sons.

We have lost when reconciliation is less important than revenge.

We have lost when hate-filled parties thirst for the blood of the Other.

We will lose, again and again, each time we choose not to confront this tortuous cycle—the cycle which itself is the ultimate enemy.

We have known loss, today.

We have lost when reconciliation is less important than revenge.

---

4 SMART POWER
Smarter, not harder

Hate leads to harm leads to loss leads to hate leads to harm leads to loss leads to hate…. This cycle is vicious and persistent. So persistent, in fact, that there can be no "spontaneous solution"—no softening of hearts—while shots are still being traded. Reconciliation is hard. Breaking the cycle requires insight and courage and humility; the same rational, compassionate and moral human guidance you will see again and again. We'll talk much more about "Mind" in the next section, but here's a primer on "smart power."

Interdependence is and ought to be as much the ideal of man as self-sufficiency. Man is a social being.
Mohandas Gandhi

On the wall of our traditional Japanese martial art (*jujutsu*) hall (*dojo*) hangs a sign:

Avoid rather than check
Check rather than hurt
Hurt rather than maim
And maim rather than kill
For all life is precious and no one has the authority to take it away

Unfortunately, the reality is that we don't have an optimal balance among American national assets.

As a member of the aforementioned dojo, a retired SEAL, and an advisor to the Department of Defense, I have to speak out for improvements to our "whole of government" campaign for national security and international engagement. We begin by acknowledging that the two are inextricably connected. Counterterrorism itself is all too often relegated to the military and other coercive organizations because the problem is popularly seen as being one of violence. It is not…not entirely. The State Department's role in *countering* terrorism should be recognized to be as important as, or more important than, military power. Unfortunately, the reality is that we don't have an optimal balance among American national assets.

The terrorist actor uses violence as a voice and as a means of influence. He manipulates the environment to manipulate minds. The real battlefield is not a horrifying five-second explosive attack, a dramatic five-minute gunfight, or an agonizing five-hour recovery of human remains. The war of terror is for the mind, and this "Long War" is truly a long one…of five years, five decades, and five generations. More importantly, resorting to terrorist behavior is an *admission of weakness*, because the user does not perceive that he holds any legitimate method of influence.

Most importantly, the extended nature of this long war is a blessing in disguise. Since most humans possess the capacity to learn and to grow, it is possible to convey to even the bitterest rivals that force-on-force problem solving is a self-defeating exercise.

The ultimate source of a threat is not the motivated attacker facing us, but more accurately his distorted thinking—he has come to see our entire family, culture or religion as his enemy. To accomplish real progress with a long view takes courage. Choosing *not* to fight, wherever and whenever alternatives exist, is courageous; actively reserving our capacity for violence is courageous. Far from being a display of weakness, this choice is a bold statement of the United States' and its allies' deep

Choosing not to fight, wherever and whenever alternatives exist, is courageous…

Secretary of Defense Robert Gates famously insisted, "We cannot kill or capture our way to victory."

---

commitment to full-spectrum global security. Secretary of Defense Robert Gates famously insisted, "We cannot kill or capture our way to victory."

Reserving the capacity for force, however, does not mean we abandon, reduce or degrade it. On the contrary, the better we refine our ability to destroy, the more evident our full range of options will be on the world stage. The more apparent our capacity to cause harm, combined with our clearly seen determination to avoid its use, the more credible will be our commitment to preventing violent conflict.

Focused violence is essential to specific situations. The most obvious example is the threat posed by a suicide bomber (PBIED, or personnel-borne IED). Quick, violent action by those threatened means the difference between their life and death and a life-or-death moment for any innocent men, women or children in the vicinity. My friend Sean Mickle remembers perching on a rooftop in Iraq and watching in slow motion as his individual bullets impacted the chest of a VBIED (vehicle-borne improvised explosive device) driver. This rolling car bomb was hurtling toward the compound housing Sean and his unit of U.S. Marine Corps "Recon" commandos. His wounding the driver resulted in a premature detonation, which may have been caused by a "dead man" switch, triggering the device when the driver's hand pulled away from the console or steering wheel. This premature detonation probably prevented a small-scale version of the 1983 Beirut bombing that killed 220 of their fellow Marines. Sean's story provides an excellent illustration of necessary violence.

Copious use of this "hard" option may seem efficient and productive. Factoring in the human cost, however, the tool can become inhumane, irresponsible and frustratingly counter-productive. Hard power casually applied can continue to harden all actors until conflict appears irreconcilable. Such a lose-lose proposition is in no one's best interests.

Conversely, "Soft" power—the term coined by Harvard's Joseph Nye in 1990—captures the dynamic of leveraging international influence by means of *attraction* and *persuasion* through appealing aspects of national culture, values and institutions. "It is the ability to get what you want through attraction rather than coercion or

According to Professor Nye, "Smart power
is the combination of the hard power of
coercion and payment with the soft power
of persuasion and attraction."

payments." (*Soft Power; The Means to Success in World Politics*, PublicAffairs, 2004)
Consider as just one example Japan, which in past decades embraced select portions
of U.S. culture (baseball, poodle skirts, Elvis) and, correspondingly, maintained
open channels through which political, military, economic and other sharing flowed
for mutual benefit.

Soft power's conceptual offspring, "smart" power, is the tailored blending of
soft (persuasive) and hard (coercive) powers for every specific situation. According
to Professor Nye, "Smart power is the combination of the hard power of coercion
and payment with the soft power of persuasion and attraction." (*The Future of Power*,
PublicAffairs, 2011). Nye and co-chair Richard Armitage further explain in the *CSIS
Commission on Smart Power; A smarter, more secure America* (Center for Strategic
and International Studies, 2007):

> "Smart power means developing an integrated strategy, resource base,
> and tool kit to achieve American objectives, drawing on both hard
> and soft power. It is an approach that underscores the necessity of a
> strong military, but also invests heavily in alliances, partnerships, and
> institutions at all levels to expand American influence and establish the
> legitimacy of American action. Providing for the global good is central
> to this effort because it helps America reconcile its overwhelming
> power with the rest of the world's interests and values."

Simply being more mindful of unintended
consequences, and exercising our ability
to speak out and act, gives individuals real
power to make a difference.

Extending Professor Nye's international relations theory of smart power to the interpersonal level, I point to the *application* of smart power as a grassroots approach for local as well as global peacemaking. Simply being more mindful of unintended consequences, and exercising our ability to speak out and act, gives individuals real power to make a difference. Think of this as *applied* smart power, or ASP, well within the reach of every concerned citizen. And without balancing closer relationships, what hope is there for improved global engagement? Like parents who overcome differences to raise a healthy family, macro-level, external conflict reduction rests on the building blocks of effective internal relationships. Ultimately, as the old hymn goes, "Let there be peace on earth...and let it begin with me."

I promised to make this a primer, and not an encyclopedic analysis of smart power. Let me keep that promise. Academic discussion never stimulates like real-world examples of a topic anyway, so let's move on to some stories of friends and foes and failures and successes in applying smart power for balanced peacemaking.

5 RESTRAINT

Cause a Pause

The cycle of harm and loss is nearly unbreakable without deliberate effort. Needless to say, this high-minded ideal can be challenging to practice when bullets, fists or words are still flying.

I tried to talk with them, but they couldn't hear me over their RPGs.

Eric Hatter

Our platoon, shortly before 9/11/01. Despite a wide range of interests and capabilities, there was an unbreakable unity of purpose.

> ## We can begin to understand what we don't understand about the other by just *saying* what we think is going on.

I want to share a favorite *The Naked Gun* (Paramount Pictures, 1988) movie exchange in which the late, great Leslie Nielsen, as Police Lt. Frank Drebin, encounters a thug sent to kill him. The assailant yells, "I have a message for ya from Vincent Ludwig!" and begins firing at Drebin. He continues, "Take that, you lousy cop!"

Frank yells back, "I'm sorry! I can't hear ya! Don't fire the gun while you're talking!"

(By the way, I strongly recommend you rent or buy *Naked Gun* for an hour and a half of delightful peacemaking…it's very hard to hate while you're laughing.)

The opening quote for this chapter is from a comment posted at our blog, PowerfulPeace.net. Eric "Madd" Hatter, a longtime friend and fellow retired SEAL, made the point that some of the concepts in Powerful Peace can seem a little unrealistic. The RPG's he mentions are the "rocket-propelled grenades" that were fired at him in Iraq. His comment is a facetious reference to my apparent desire to hold hands with terrorists/insurgents and sing Kumbaya.

While on the surface he appears to oppose my position outright, I couldn't be more pleased to have this counterpoint expressed so succinctly. It's exactly why frank dialogue is important. "We" (Rob and Eric, or The West and The East, or any other We and They) can begin to understand what we don't understand about the other by just *saying* what we think is going on. That opens the exchange of information, which begins to clear up dangerous misunderstandings.

Yes, sometimes you gotta shoot a guy.

The message of Powerful Peace is not to attempt reasoning with an insurgent who is aiming an RPG at me. In that moment, there is only one option if I hope to see kith and kin again. By now you can imagine what it is.

Powerful Peace isn't "either-or." Either-or is the enemy of Powerful Peace, because it says such things as, "*either* you claim my religion—*or* I can kill you;" "*either* you're in my political party—*or* I can't respect you."

…"*Either* you're with us…*or* you're against us."

If changing the entire world is a bridge too far, we can at least nibble around the edges of bitter conflict...

In contrast, responsible living is more appropriately an "all," as in accepting "all options" available for a particular situation. Builders are masters at selecting the right tool for each job. A hammer will drive home a screw, but poorly. And I could probably, eventually, drive in a nail with a screwdriver—but I'd need some aspirin afterward!

I'll use the dialogue tool to engage the community that breeds the guy that wants to kill me with an RPG. Ultimately, the idea is to engage with communities that don't yet even have guys that want to kill me with an RPG. For example, I would love to reach a *potential* "guy with the RPG" while he's a child, years before his radicalization, and help his family help him become an engineer, a physician, or a musician instead of an insurgent. If changing the entire world is a bridge too far, we can at least nibble around the edges of bitter conflict; one person, family or neighborhood at a time.

As I wrote in an essay entitled "Becoming Your Enemy" in 2005, "The next evolution of terrorist threat mitigation is elimination, *before* the hateful cause exists, by working with the source." We have to learn to operate in the "space" referred to by Viktor Frankl and championed by Stephen R. Covey: "Between stimulus and response there is a space. In that space is our power to choose our response. In our response lie our growth and our freedom." (*7 Habits of Highly Effective People,* Free Press, 1990.) In other words, I can react to others according to old habits and assumptions...or I can try to understand what's going on, and respond in a manner much more likely to move me toward my true goals.

In military planning we often refer to enemy and friendly groups as Red forces and Blue forces, respectively. Appropriately, a third color is sometimes used to describe those locals resident in a conflict area who are not willingly allied with either faction. This great majority of those among whom an insurgency or war swirls, these moms and dads, kids and grandpas, is called "Green" forces. (Note: sometimes "local nationals"—i.e., Afghans in Afghanistan—are subdivided into White, for neutral civilians, and Green, for official local military or government personnel. Philosophies differ; I prefer to simplify this for ease of reading.)

**For too long, we have given only passing notice
to the human beings suffering amid hostilities.**

Green is an interesting selection, considering how other bloody games (viz. rugby) are also fought on a green expanse.

For too long, we have given only passing notice to the human beings suffering amid hostilities. Seeing little more than a burden of humanitarian needs, we have frequently failed to recognize this living backdrop as a key component of our operational success or failure.

Nowadays, however, insightful commanders are changing the paradigm. Major General Mike Flynn, former Deputy Chief of Staff (Intelligence) for the International Security Assistance Force (ISAF) in Afghanistan, published a paper entitled *"Fixing Intel; A Blueprint for Making Intelligence Relevant in Afghanistan"* with the Center for a New American Security (CNAS, 2010).

In this clarion call he declares that we have relied on kinetic (offensive) operations too heavily, neglecting to study and understand the host population. This does *not* mean we should abandon kinetic capacity. As you're reading throughout Powerful Peace, you'll also find in *Fixing Intel* that the ability to fight and to kill is essential. Yet you will also read about a "...tendency to overemphasize detailed information about the enemy at the expense of the political, economic, and cultural environment that supports it...."

In other words, the lives and needs and interests of people among whom we are fighting have not been factored in adequately to even support *our own* best interests.

From that same document, we read the quoted guidance of General Stanley McChrystal, then-commander of ISAF: "The conflict will be won by persuading the population, not by destroying the enemy." In my advisory capacity I often point to the fact that Red actors are simply former Green citizens who have crossed into

...the lives and needs and interests of people among whom we are fighting have not been factored in adequately to even support *our own* best interests.

our enemy's camp. (In some cases, an individual is literally Green by day and Red by night.) And *again*, this crossing over is always caused by some perceived need or grievance, whether due to economic constraints or a desire for revenge. If we are able to effectively address these, therefore, we stand to gain. Every increase to the ranks of Green forces reduces the Red by one.

Consider the practical effects of this large group on both friendly and enemy efforts: the human aspect of life, or HAL, is a powerful motivator. In difficult situations it can override cultural biases and swing a local population toward either side. On a sports field, the turf stays quietly in place. It stays level. Not so with dynamic, feeling, human terrain.

The "Green forces" human terrain rises up to shelter our enemy when he is the lesser of evils, and it channels us in the right direction when he is not. Our footing is closely connected to and dependent upon its inclination.

The vast, green field is as real, and as necessary, as any other planning factor for our eventual victory in armed conflict...the fact that we just might help save some kids in the process is of course a pretty tasty gravy.

Powerful Peace is apolitical. We can learn to grow beyond blind adherence to ideology. No single party holds a monopoly on making a safer world for all our families. Once a person understands our mutual responsibility to one another and the goodwill it can engender, she can begin to exercise the CAP, that cause-a-pause option, for the greater good of our species and herself. Remember: we don't have to "like" each other in order to "accept" one another. Every human is a stakeholder, and *every* one of us is a potential agent of peace.

No single party holds a monopoly on making a safer world for all our families.

---

6 ALTERNATIVES
I won't make my wife a prostitute

What will any man do when faced with a range of unacceptable choices? He'll select the least lousy option and proceed accordingly. It may be that violent crime is the only game in town. But what if more appealing alternatives could be provided, at little expense to the providers? The reach and reward of generous thinking holds great promise. Like all ASP solutions, this is a Return on Investment that pays the investor in improved personal security. We need to invest in solutions.

This whole thing sucks, you know?
I mean, it all coulda been avoided so incredibly easy....
To shame a man like that, and back him into a corner;
seems to me that some*thing* is out of whack, not some*one*.
"Jim Palumbo"

The title for this chapter was born during a conversation at the American embassy outpost in Basra, Iraq. It was quoted by an Iraqi friend, the senior cultural advisor to our diplomats there. He was passing me a comment from another friend out in town, a *Baswari* (Basra resident) who was not—not yet—fighting on the side of the insurgency: "I won't make my wife a prostitute."

This Baswari was one of thousands of unemployed Iraqi men, living in pathetic conditions with unemployment several times greater than the U.S. experienced at the height of its recent recession. He needed work, because his family needed food.

Appropriately, we will capture or kill this now-valid enemy "target," this pitiful actor at the end of his rope...

He told my friend the options were simple: 1) acquire gainful employment; 2) put his wife to work as a hooker; 3) emplace an improvised explosive device (IED, or "roadside bomb") to earn the freelance insurgent "supporter" rate of $150—and thus feed his family for a month.

On point 1, with nearly 30% unemployment (70% in some areas, and 80% for women), he had no opportunities. On point 2, he had taken a stand. Door number 3 remained the only avenue. If our soldier is killed by the IED he emplaces, what will our response be? Appropriately, we will capture or kill this now-valid enemy "target," this pitiful actor at the end of his rope, this family's only possible breadwinner...greatly worsening the situation of a woman and children already in desperate need. Via video feeds, I've watched live as men were disintegrated by our costly missiles—adding another expense to this spiraling drama—and wondered at their stories. How many would have fit into this scenario of desperate choices? Final tally in such a tragically unnecessary scenario: one dead American, one dead Iraqi, and two families in two hemispheres torn apart.

The slain bomber's neighbors will long remember the circumstances in the neighborhood, the fate of this man, and the consequent suffering of his family. The cycle will continue.

For years I've written and spoken about the urgent need for individuals and populations with dominant power to look through the eyes of other individuals and populations. More deliberate, more pervasive engagement is a systematic way of reducing conflict on all sides. If this is the era of the "social network," we should probably put away old patterns of isolation and fear; so many opportunities exist to learn about the Other. Again in the words of Stephen R. Covey (*Principle-Centered Leadership*, Fireside, 1992):

More deliberate, more pervasive engagement is a systematic way of reducing conflict on all sides.

It's not hard to imagine the shame and anger
of men who cannot satisfy their families' needs.

"If you want to overcome the pull of the past—those powerful restraining forces of habit, custom, and culture—to bring about desired change, count the costs and rally the necessary resources. In the space program, we see that tremendous thrust is needed to clear the powerful pull of the earth's gravity. So it is with breaking old habits."

The struggles we prevent can range from passive-aggressive hassles in the workplace, to taking an unwelcome knife in the ribs, to wars between states based on trembling platforms of misinformation, ignorance, paranoia and reaction.

Let me offer just one highly preferable alternative to killing a man who puts out an IED to kill an American to earn $150 to give his daughter some food: if he contracts to not take hostile action against our forces, let's give him $300 to subsist for one month. That's right; let's double his income, giving him a one-time, good-deal payout of $300 to care for his family as he chooses. There's only one condition; that he not participate in attacks against our forces or his own struggling government. He'll be made to understand this with crystal clarity: any violation of the agreement will yield radically amplified legal, and perhaps lethal, consequences. With such an agreement, and for the potential gain to all parties, I'd write this check from my own family's accounts!

In the next month, let's offer him the same $300—only this time, we'll attach a string: he has to sit through vocational rehabilitation classes to learn a trade like electrical work. Heaven knows, shattered nations are in desperate need of qualified electricians to begin patching together a safe and reliable infrastructure. The hazards of electrocution, and the certainty of regular electrical failures, are common risks in Iraq.

The third month, let's attach another string to receive $300: he'll accompany a master electrician as an apprentice in town, reinforcing the lessons he learned in his classes. His compensation now includes not only double pay for greatly reduced risk, but also the experience for a new career, the self-esteem of providing for his family, the peace of mind of household economic security and the stabilization of his local neighborhood.

Equally important to their families and neighbors, they rediscover self-respect.

(It's not hard to imagine the shame and anger of men who cannot satisfy their families' needs. For a vivid illustration of the extremes to which a man may be driven, watch Denzel Washington in *John Q* (New Line Cinema, 2002). John Q's friend, Jim, spoke the great line I used as the intro to this chapter. "This whole thing sucks, you know? I mean, it all coulda been avoided so incredibly easy." Do we really want to be looking back over the next, bloody, intercultural conflict and find ourselves saying the same thing *after* lives and limbs have been lost?)

The fourth month, and every month afterward, our participant will be required to earn his $300 by working as an instructor-electrician and escorting new apprentices coming up through the same program.

The fifth month, we can begin to split the salary cost, with the host government's paying half and preparing to assume what is ultimately a domestic responsibility.

Within half a year, starting in month six, the local national government should bear the entire, minimal, cost of these salaries in exchange for improved public power distribution and a reduction in injuries/mishaps caused by faulty wiring. No coalition soldier is killed by the men in this program, because they receive twice the income for a safe and rewarding occupation. Equally important to their families and neighbors, they rediscover self-respect. No wife is pimped, no child is hungry, and the rebuilding of a society is in full swing. We hold the leverage and authority of the original work contract, and his understanding of doubled or tripled punishment for violating it.

The scheme describes an electrician as its subject, but struggling countries have equally urgent needs for masons, plumbers, builders, and more. Reconstructing the infrastructure becomes a growth industry itself, building up a growing network of local economies, made up of service and goods providers, manufacturers, and clients.

Reconstructing the infrastructure becomes a growth industry itself, building up a growing network of local economies...

Real, unlimited solutions in the unlimited world of conflict are within reach...

How could these costs work out, you ask? Well, according to conservative estimates at the time the subtitle-quote was spoken, the U.S. government alone paid more than ten billion dollars a *month* to run the war in Iraq. Two years later, the cost in Afghanistan was about the same. If we round that total down for argument's sake to nine billion, the proposed $300 monthly wage rate could extend to *thirty million work-study program participants.*

Of course, each country only has about thirty million citizens altogether....

Obviously, we're not going to stop paying for bombs, bullets and butter. So let's divert just one thousandth of those nine billion dollars, and begin rebuilding the nation with 30,000 men. Or take just one *ten-thousandth* (0.01%, or $900,000) and start with "only" 3,000. That's *3,000* families stabilized, *3,000* potential bombers prevented, and 3,000 fewer chances for our soldier to be torn apart. He will be more likely to return safely to his own beloved family. Imagine where this could take us.

But where would we find less than one million dollars to spare? Well, you could start by cutting out the gourmet ice cream cart at my dining facility (DFAC). My comrades and I will find some way to bravely carry on without creamy delights smothered in luscious toppings. It is a war, after all. And that's a small personal price to pay to reduce the number of desperate men and buried bombs.

Real, unlimited solutions in the unlimited world of conflict are within reach, if we are willing to use imagination, daring, and the vast reservoir of experience held by security professionals and policy makers who refuse to get back into the box.

7   SELF-INTEREST
Simple Needs

Why did you do the first thing you did this morning? My guess is that was driven by a physical urging to head for a certain room of the house. But why did you do the second thing you did? Was it starting the coffee, or the heater, or the television? This was driven by self-interest. Those are obvious examples, but think through to some action less obvious; how about the first thing someone else "made" you do? Did you go to school, work or chores? That would have been based on self-interest, too. You may have wanted to avoid a scolding, or losing a paycheck. Every conscious choice is based on some personally "preferred" outcome, even when we can't immediately recognize it as preferable.

> **Each of us has an opportunity to play a far**
> **more apparent role than at first glance,**
> **and to do so individually as well as collectively,**
> **and not to leave such matters to others or to chance alone.**
> *Jonas Salk*

Leafing through an issue of *The Counter Terrorist* magazine (Security Solutions International, May 2010), I read an excellent piece entitled "*Agent of Influence in Undercover Operations.*" Bill Majcher wrote that during his decades undercover in law enforcement, gaining the confidence of some of the most unsavory characters

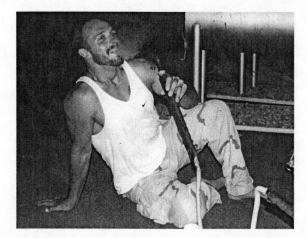

Sure, we worked hard, but relaxing later with hummus, Arabic tunes and our own, private hookah bar was ample reward. (Not all examples of self-interest look so much like the shameless self-indulgence pictured here.)

on the planet, he always reached his target through that simplest of influence tools: self-interest.

Bam. If you replace Majcher's agenda of "exploiting human greed for apprehension purposes" with one of "exploring common ground for peacemaking purposes," you'll find the overlaid approach to be nearly identical. I've spoken with Bill and CT Mag's Editor Chris Graham about these commonalities.

Understanding motivators is a powerful, universal principle of influence. The Undercover Operations article insists that individuals—all individuals—base all their decisions on self-interest.

Perhaps your mind is blurting out, "Say it isn't so! What about Mother Teresa?" Well, what about her? I say Mother Teresa was in fact motivated by the deepest of self-interest...as was Adolf Hitler.

Granted, their interests diverged radically. (That's an understatement.) She was unable to sit by while millions suffered and died. He, on the other hand, was unable to *tolerate* the peaceful existence of millions. Beneath it all, we find the same driving force: what mattered (self-interest) to these larger than life figures ended up being where they chose to invest their energy. It's the same for each of us.

Understanding motivators is a powerful, universal principle of influence.

...in Iraq and Afghanistan, I've witnessed countless examples of self-interest driving otherwise unnatural behaviors.

The thug who robs a couple on the street is no more selfish than the frightened husband who steps between the thief and his wife. One is selfish enough to steal property at the material and emotional expense of his victims. The other is selfish enough to deny his own well-being in order to protect his lady. He prefers to risk death rather than see her harmed.

In this sense, self-interest is neither good nor bad—do we judge the need to eat as "good" or "bad?"—it simply is what it is. This basic human motivator is a powerful aid in guiding human behavior.

During my recent years in Iraq and Afghanistan, I've witnessed countless examples of self-interest driving otherwise unnatural behaviors. As mentioned previously, some of the roadside bombs that kill and cripple American soldiers are placed by husbands and fathers at the end of their rope. They need money. There is no alternative financial source for basic survival.

Let me repeat that for dramatic effect: there is no alternative financial source for basic survival.

Many of these men do not desire to harm our fighters. Each is simply forced to choose between his son and mine. The answer is clear; the choice is obvious. In the United States and other stable nations, a desperate father can turn to assistance through unemployment insurance, welfare payments, or homeless shelters. For thousands of desperate fathers in Iraq, Afghanistan and elsewhere, again—there is no alternative financial source for basic survival.

Try to comprehend what you would be willing to do to ensure your family's very survival. Now consider what opportunities this gives those of us who have resources. It takes very little to help people who have nothing. If that help deters IEDs or hatreds that blossom into terrorism, isn't it a pretty good investment?

Try to comprehend what you would be willing to do to ensure your family's very survival.

Consider an example from Michael Yon, former Special Forces soldier, combat journalist, and author of *Moment of Truth in Iraq* (Richard Vigilante Books, 2008):

"When the compromises negotiated by Petraeus expired, many of the ex-professors and administrators at Mosul University lost their jobs permanently. The retired and disenfranchised military—who had helped keep the growing insurgency at bay—were now told they wouldn't be part of the new Iraq, in direct contradiction to promises made by commanders on the ground. The most able and dangerous men in the country learned they could not trust American military commanders. *Trust, the first and most important hill on the moral high ground, and we had abandoned it.* Unable to support their families, cut off from their own country's future, furious at the new regime that had made them pariahs, these men were an insurgency waiting to happen. They did not wait for long." [Italics mine]

If we just think ahead a little, such mind-bogglingly negative consequences can be avoided. Anyone reading this should be able to put himself into the shoes of one of the men Michael describes, and easily imagine how he would be impacted by the same circumstances.

Also from *Moment of Truth in Iraq*: "General Petraeus has pointed out for a long time that there is no purely military solution to the fighting in Iraq." Sounds a bit like Defense Secretary Gates' aforementioned, "We cannot kill or capture our way to victory," right? It's no coincidence that they both sound like the assertion in Powerful Peace that we have to balance hard and soft powers to have any worthwhile effect.

Now I'm going to jump the tracks just a little to wrap up with another important passage from Michael's book. Later on in Powerful Peace you'll read a chapter entitled, "It's the children, stupid." Here's a taste of the same compassion to be found in *Moment of Truth in Iraq*:

Trust, the first and most important hill on the moral high ground, and we had abandoned it.

...they will cancel the mission to get the kid to an American aid station, which, technically, they shouldn't be doing.

"American soldiers can't take it when they see a kid get burned. If they are in the neighborhood on a mission and they see a burned kid, they will cancel the mission to get the kid to an American aid station, which, technically, they shouldn't be doing. But a lot of tough soldiers get weak knee'd when they see a kid in trouble. They'll shoot insurgents all day and all night and can't get enough of it, but when they see a kid hurt, they'll stop and drive off with the kid. Thousands upon thousands of these obviously spontaneous actions had a profound effect on how the Iraqis see us. They knew we did a lot of stupid and overbearing things, even brutal and criminal things at times. But they also could not deny that, on the whole, our people had a heart for them, or at least for their kids. And who couldn't like Iraqi kids? Practically everywhere the kids loved to see the soldiers, and the soldiers loved to see the kids."

You may think this is simplistic. It is. To ensure our own best interests, global engagement must include such thinking alongside arms and sanctions. If we absolutely must hate and kill each other over stupid disagreements, let's at least make sure it's based on "reasonable" and time-tested animosities...like politics and religion. Let's do our best to make sure a father is never again killed for being unable to feed his children.

8 DIGNITY
The ugly American

International relations, like interpersonal relations, have amazing ups and downs. With the discovery and killing of Osama bin Laden in Pakistan, the situation between the U.S. and this "partner" in the war on terror degraded quickly. It will not remain so, as a glance at the last century (and reconciliation with mortal enemies Japan, Germany, Russia…) will confirm. Here, then, I'll use citizens of the nation of Pakistan to demonstrate the universal value of basic dignity in peacemaking.

**America is a Nation with a mission—and that
mission comes from our most basic beliefs.
We have no desire to dominate, no ambitions of empire.
Our aim is a democratic peace—a peace founded
upon the dignity and rights of every man and woman.**
George W. Bush

Do you remember the film, *"Blackhawk Down"* (Revolution Studios, 2001)? Probably.

Do you remember farther back, when the 1993 Mogadishu incident with U.S. Army Rangers and Special Forces troops first occurred, and we lost 18 men, some of whose bodies were desecrated? Possibly.

Do you remember the 24 Pakistani peacekeepers who were massacred in the same town just three months before the "Blackhawk Down" events?

> We tend to notice those things which affect our own.
> Thus I want to help enlarge the meaning of "our own."

Not bloody likely.

If this equally tragic occurrence sounds unfamiliar, it's probably not because you are heartless, bigoted or self-absorbed. We tend to notice those things which affect our own. Thus I want to help enlarge the meaning of "our own." If I am in fact a person, then my own kind includes all people. If we can look beyond skin and wardrobe, we will find much more to agree on and, simultaneously, less to fight about.

I deployed to Somalia on the heels of the horrible deaths and mutilations of our soldiers. We didn't experience any such combat drama afterward, of course. The U.S. pulled out of Somalia a few weeks later. What I want to emphasize is that even so soon after these two similar battles, we on the ground in Mogadishu were far more aware of the loss of 18 Americans than of those 24 Pakistanis.

Do you know who rolled on into the "Blackhawk Down" battle to conduct a large part of the rescue of our desperate American forces in Mogadishu? Pakistani soldiers.

Fast forward eight years, and you'll find me conducting reconnaissance to facilitate the invasion of Afghanistan soon after 9/11. Pakistani soldiers were responsible for escorting us and providing security while we conducted our business.

We didn't come under fire that day. If we had, there is a fair chance some of them would have been wounded or killed defending our lives.

As I entered the U.S. DFAC for dinner at a base in Baghdad one evening, I was met by three large posters on the wall emphasizing the importance of Equal Opportunity. These were produced to express the official policy of the military toward prejudicial behavior.

At the top of each was the title, "Equal Opportunity," and at the bottom were "DIGNITY and RESPECT" in large, bold, rainbow-colored letters.

One poster gave definitions for the categories of Racial, Gender and Religious discrimination. Below these, it said forcefully, "Not in our Army!"

Once I had made my way to the food line, I had the distinct displeasure of watching an American soldier as he scowled at the Pakistani food server behind the counter and waited petulantly for his order to be followed to the letter. He had three Styrofoam take-out containers and had ordered three different meals for buddies.

It quickly became obvious that this was a real SOB. By SOB, of course, I mean Strategically Off Base. Such SOBs are shining examples of the "ugly American" reputation. They can be big, rude, and with a revolting sense of entitlement when dealing with sometimes smaller, sometimes darker people, for whom English may be a second language. Given the right opportunities, SOBs have an amazing super power: they can sour neutral or even positive attitudes of foreign nationals toward the United States.

This American stared at the server with open contempt. While the flustered man tried to make sense of his complicated instructions, the SOB simply glared, making no effort to clarify the request. Once the server completed the first two meals and hustled off to get a bun for the third, the soldier snatched up two containers and walked away up the line, forcing the server to hasten to catch up.

As the Pakistani man rushed up with this final meal, the SOB just glared at him again and snarled, "I said *barbecue* sandwich!"

I won't soon forget that quote. In a movie, it would have been funny; spoken by the guy nobody's supposed to like who always loses the girl in the end. He said it in a tone a mean child might use with a small dog. The petty comment reminded me of some in the comfortable headquarters staff at war who will bitch that the DFAC's Baskin-Robbins ice cream server doesn't have a particular flavor one day…while fellow soldiers at remote outposts grind into a thirty-fourth day with nothing but cold MREs (Meal, Ready to Eat).

After the SOB strutted away, apparently satisfied that he had put that little so-and-so in his place, I apologized to the server for the disgraceful behavior and told him some Americans think they're kings.

A bomb tech sergeant next to me shook his head and said, "You got that right," as he watched the SOB stalk off.

Two thoughts:

To the Pakistani soldiers who gave their lives, risked their lives, and protected my life with theirs: Thank you. *Shukriya.*

It quickly became obvious that this was a real SOB. By SOB, of course, I mean Strategically Off Base.

It doesn't matter how hard our leadership tries to teach, if you choose not to learn. Bite the bullet on the fear and frustration of war—for your own future benefit.

To the SOB: Grow up. It doesn't matter how hard our leadership tries to teach, if you choose not to learn. Bite the bullet on the fear and frustration of war—for your own future benefit. I know how hard it hurts to lose your buddies. Believe me. But try to comprehend that your well-being is tied to that of others. Show some Dignity and Respect—become a participant in our struggle for genuine global security. It will never make things better to abuse more innocent bystanders.

9 RESPECT
Guarding killers at Abu Ghraib prison

I conducted a week's antiterrorism assessment at Abu Ghraib prison outside Baghdad not long after the prisoner abuse scandal raged through the global media. I was taught a humbling lesson in the value of humble respect.

Without feelings of respect, what is there to distinguish men from beasts?
Confucius

As in most of the assessment visits we conducted worldwide, my team found many well-intentioned young service members at Abu Ghraib, doing the best they could

Some murals from the walls of the prison's main chamber; barred cells below massive images of the beloved, murdering dictator.

They faced each day knowing it might be their last...and carried away the broken bodies of their comrades when that time came for them.

with the challenge set before them at the military detention center. Soldiers went about their 12-hour work days in the blazing sun, no weekends, for months on end. They put their heads down when the rocket attacks came, and stepped back out to work when the rocket attacks concluded. They faced each day knowing it might be their last...and carried away the broken bodies of their comrades when that time came for them. I recall at least one near fatality among the several IDF ("indirect fire," or rocket and mortar) events we experienced that week.

As extraordinary as this lifestyle may sound to some readers, it is common for hundreds of thousands of U.S. soldiers and for millions of others around the world. It's because of the rigors of their lifestyle, and the callousness you might expect it to engender, that I was especially humbled by a simple lesson of insight shared by one facility guard I interviewed.

Swaggering in my "cammie" uniform, rifle and Trident (SEAL insignia patch), I'd been looking out over The Yard enclosed in triple-strand concertina wire while we talked and staring at the detainees with self-righteous, angry suspicion. Which one had most recently killed one of my own friends? I asked this guard how he could stand to deal with these (my word) "scumbags."

"I just try to treat them all with respect," he replied. "Some of these men were detained for being in the wrong place at the wrong time. They're innocent, but it'll take us several *months* to confirm that and return them to their families." He paused. "It's hard, here, for a woman to try to run the house without her husband." I deflated a little.

He continued, "Some are absolutely guilty. That guy over there," he pointed to a smallish, quiet, ordinary-looking individual walking alone in a *dishdasha* robe, "killed two Americans in an ambush a few days ago. He's a hard case and nobody else can work with him. But he's willing to talk with me, and usually does what I ask. I think it's because I act respectfully toward him." I deflated the rest of the way.

Respect is sometimes a feeling we get when we admire someone. Like the feeling of "love," however, this form of respect is an involuntary response and can't be controlled. Many people had feelings of respect for Hitler, based on his awesome

We can offer respect to anyone, even to an
enemy, and this choice can make our jobs,
our environment, and even our life easier.

power to destroy. What this guard reminded me, on the other hand, is that the *verb* "to respect" (like the verb "to love") is available to us at any time, regardless of our feelings. We can offer respect to anyone, even to an enemy, and this choice can make our jobs, our environment, and even our life easier.

We can't always know a person's entire situation. Wait, scratch that. We can't *ever* know a person's entire situation. I might look out into a sandy prison compound enclosed in multiple strands of eviscerating wire and find myself glaring contemptuously at…a florist. Or I might be contempting some young humanitarian, some future democratic leader of his society, whose pleas of innocence sound just too good to be true.

On the other hand, I might in fact be looking straight at an honest-to-goodness, cold blooded killer, someone who recently took the life of one of my comrades. Even in this extreme case, however, I have to examine my own intentions and actual self-interest (remember that term?) and act accordingly. Is demeaning treatment from me likely to build further resistance and thus interfere with my purposes? Is the immediate satisfaction of getting back at someone worth the loss of my long-term goals? Whether my intention is to gain compliance from a prisoner, negotiate a better price with a wily shopkeeper, or simply work out the optimal division of chores around my household, some wise old guy somewhere in history probably said it best when he first declared, "You get more flies with honey than with vinegar."

Is the immediate satisfaction of getting back at
someone worth the loss of my long-term goals?

10 GRIEVANCE
Terrorism is only a tool

With the "War on Terror" we declared war on a TACTIC. We declared war on a METHOD. We may as well have declared a War to Eliminate Ambushes or a War to Eliminate Sniper Fire. I was one of those earliest Warriors on Terror, and I'm equally guilty of having missed the bigger picture during the passionate early years following 9/11. Terrorism can be used by—and is used by—aggrieved individuals of every nation, faith, and color. We should update the world's understanding about terrorism: it is far, far more effective and economical to "fight" violent extremism by preventing it.

**In this small world, we must realize that
our neighbor's troubles are also our own.**
Oscar Arias Sanchez

The primary focus of this book is on reducing conflict and, by extension, terrorism. Terrorism is less an inevitable horror, and more a useful method for effecting some desired change in others. I mentioned earlier that the use of terrorism is an admission of weakness. Because terrorists lack more legitimate means of influence, they settle for violent spectacle. Each of us, by virtue of our birth into the human race, is eminently qualified to understand much about this destructive and despicable behavior. Its origins are firmly rooted in human nature.

Because terrorists lack more legitimate means
of influence, they settle for violent spectacle.

I've spent years engaged in counterterrorism. In various roles I've been tasked with "becoming" our adversary for the purpose of envisioning and advising an effective defense. I've studied terrorists with the purpose of understanding them—as a sympathetic insider. Terrorists share one thing in common with every other human being on earth: human nature.

Humans seek a secure, satisfying condition. It's unnatural, exhausting, and miserable to devote your life to unconscionable violence...unless some other unacceptable imbalance in your life compels it. This refers back to underlying grievances.

We'll always have some need of combat power, as some adversaries will always threaten violence. But some defensive energy is aimed in the wrong direction. If we can affect the *sources* of terrorism in proactive ways, we can reduce our dependence (and our expenditures, each of which represents a small victory for the terrorist) on endlessly improved defenses and rising costs for force-based supremacy. We can avoid playing into the hands of enemies like the late Osama bin Laden, who boasted that one of his tactics was to count on the cost of wars to bankrupt the United States.

On the subject of bin Laden, there is no more recognized authority than Peter Bergen, CNN's National Security Analyst. Author of *The Osama bin Laden I Know* (Free Press, 2006) and his latest, *The Longest War: The Enduring Conflict Between America and al-Qaeda* (Free Press, 2011), Peter is one of the few Western journalists in the world to have interviewed the founder of al Qaeda face-to-face. He provides insights unavailable to purely theoretical analysts of the ugly real world of this group and its former leader. In *Holy War, Inc.* (Touchstone, 2001) he addressed the issue of actual terrorist motivations:

In various roles I've been tasked with
"becoming" our adversary for the purpose of
envisioning and advising an effective defense.

"Why is bin Laden doing what he is doing? To attempt an answer, we have to refrain from caricature and instead attend to bin Laden's own statements about why he is at war with the United States....

"Of all the tens of thousands of words that bin Laden has uttered on the public record there are some significant omissions: he does not rail against the pernicious effects of Hollywood movies, or against Madonna's midriff, or against the pornography protected by the U.S. Constitution....

"Bin Laden is at war with the United States, but his is a political war, justified by his own understanding of Islam, and directed at the symbols and institutions of American power....

"In addition, treating 'Islam' as a monolith defies common sense. There are as many Islams as there are Christianities."

I say Amen to that final observation, especially. My own pastor in a Presbyterian church once told me that not only were other religions—Hinduism; Islam—"cults" and therefore bound for the fiery pit, but that other so-called Christian traditions—Baptist; Methodist—are as well. And not only those, but *other Presbyterian branches* were similarly wrong-headed and deserved any ultimate punishment as may befall them.

Whether its intent is to restructure a government, repel a foreign force, or acquire some other accommodation, the raw material of terrorism (terror) is merely a method of persuasion; a voice. Some people choose actual words as their voice. Some choose the expression of political power. Some, called terrorists, seek to change an unacceptable situation by force. Behind this choice, in every, single case, is some perceived grievance.

Sometimes the solution to a grievance is within easy reach. It only requires awareness of the problem; in my hometown, if I see that ten dollars I'll never miss can relieve the hunger of a family for a day, my options are reduced by compassion—to one.

Recognizing that grievances can sometimes be relieved by simple awareness of the lives of our neighbors brings a responsibility. If we can easily solve stubborn

---

...the raw material of terrorism (terror) is
merely a method of persuasion; a voice.

...how far might the ripples extend from our best attempts to satisfy little needs?

pain points, we should. How many thousands of little needs could be satisfied by redirecting the development costs of one missile system? How many generations of new missile systems, on the other hand, might we need to buy because we disregard little needs?

If we do try, how far might the ripples extend from our best attempts to satisfy little needs? How many others might be inspired to take little steps based on this example? Either choice can lead to self-fulfilling prophecy. Either choice can initiate a cycle of behavior. Isn't it time we chose little needs first, before new long-range missiles? Time we chose new cycles of help and trust over the cycles of hate and suspicion?

If we address the elephant in the room called "grievance" and discover the keys to reducing misunderstanding and miscommunication; if we reduce the retaliation that springs from a poorly handled today; if we rewrite our future by learning from our past, then how many of our own loved ones might be invisibly spared from that threat in years to come?

11 RESILIENCE
Thank You, Mr. bin Laden

While I was still in uniform, I once had what's called a "bad landing." That's what happens when a SEAL gets into an airplane just fine and jumps out of it just fine, but then experiences a less-than-optimal reunion with the planet. The spinal surgery and other consequences of this event offer an excellent segue to discuss the in-validity of the use of terror.

> **You all know that I have been sustained**
> **throughout my life by three saving graces—**
> **my family, my friends, and a faith in**
> **the power of resilience and hope.**
> **These graces have carried me through**
> **difficult times and they have**
> **brought more joy to the good times**
> **than I ever could have imagined.**
> *Elizabeth Edwards*

Achilles died.

We'll get back to that in a moment.

As a result of the above parachuting mishap, a surgeon sliced into my throat and shoved my trachea, esophagus and artery out of the way in order to gouge out a damaged disc from my spine. Earlier in the same operation, he had carved bone

With close friend and Teammate Shaun Keilen in the weeks before 9/11/01. In this photo you can just make out the scar below the shadow on my throat that will be explained, below.

out of my hip and fashioned a replacement, which he now fit into my spine. He capped this all off by screwing a titanium plate into the vertebrae above and below the replacement, then zipped up my throat.

When the entire production was finally healed, it turned out to be exactly as the surgeon had promised: the neck was not only good as new, but stronger than before. With those two vertebrae fused into one, there is a negligible reduction of flexibility, but a generally reinforced structure. In other words, I could endure the same fall better now, thanks to this invasive and gruesome process, than with my original neck.

Achilles died.

Again, we'll get back to that in a moment.

Osama bin Laden was no Superman. His image may have become more familiar than those of some legitimate world leaders. No matter. He was a living myth, blown up by the real affection of a handful of admirers and an unreal mystique for millions, awed by the attacks accomplished at his instigation.

OBL must have sometimes gotten diarrhea. He must have had uncomfortable and embarrassing gassy moments, and he must have sometimes gotten a little booger on the outside of his nostril. How do I know this? Because he was human. When I teach students to "think like the terrorist" I urge them to first put the adversary into perspective. To esteem him unrealistically is to self-inflict intimidation. It is to give weight and energy to *his* cause, to the detriment of our own. They're only guys, guys.

Bin Laden and AQ acted as a malevolent surgeon on the spine of the free world. With 9/11 they sliced into a global throat in hopes of finding the jugular to kill the patient.

When I teach students to "think like the terrorist" I urge them to first put the adversary into perspective. To esteem him unrealistically is to self-inflict intimidation.

They failed.

Before I "broke my neck a little bit," my neck was natural and average. After the surgery I was sore for some months of healing. In the end, my spine was technically (but not noticeably) less flexible. It was also greatly reinforced, better able to survive trauma similar to what had caused the original damage.

After the "operation" of 9/11, the patient (the world) was sore for a few months of healing. The patient was understandably anxious about the future and the prognosis for recovery. To the unacknowledged disappointment of the surviving 9/11 attack supporters and their McQaeda franchises worldwide, however, the end result is the same as my own surgery. These attacks did not kill the patient. The operation steeled a spine. Our world is stronger, and better prepared, to meet malevolent actors in the future.

Achilles is remembered as a great Greek warrior who was invulnerable except for one small spot on his heel. During the news footage filmed as the attacks occurred, we can still hear one commentator's anguished remark, spoken in the heat of that desperate moment: terrorists had "found the Achilles' heel of America." This was an inaccurate analogy.

Achilles died.

America and the world we share and serve together, however, are stronger than ever before.

Thank you, Mr. bin Laden.

12 ACCOUNTABILITY

Pop Quiz: Do we make our misfortune?

The Golden Rule, karma, what-goes-around-comes-around, just desserts, paying it forward…the list of universal human expressions for consequence seems endless. Yet century after century we find ourselves relearning the same lessons our parents and ancient sages tried to teach before. Maybe it's time to really learn this lesson, for our own good.

Everybody, soon or late, sits down to a banquet of consequences.
Robert Louis Stevenson

Pop Quiz:

1. I drove my car while drunk, and I was pulled over and arrested. Who is to blame for the detention and corresponding fines that turned out to be a serious hassle for me?

    a) Society is

    b) My parents are

    c) I am

    d) Those meddling cops are

2. I poured a kettle of boiling water over my leg, then suddenly experienced severe pain and some blistering. Who is to blame for this gross injustice?

    a) The people at the water company are

    b) The manufacturers of the kettle with inadequate safety markings are

c) I am

d) Those meddling cops are

3. I stomped into a foreign country, demanding that the strange looking people there treat me special because I'm an American and everyone should just deal with it. Amazingly, the locals began to act disrespectfully toward me and I quickly realized they were starting to serve me a little slower, a little less enthusiastically, and sometimes even without a smile. Who is responsible for this outrage?

a) The local national President or Prime Minister is

b) The stupid local population is

c) I am

d) Those meddling cops are!

If you answered 1—c; 2—c; and 3—c, you got a perfect score!

It's not cliché to say that "what goes around comes around." Actually, I suppose that is a cliché. But clichés are often based on some objective reality. Obviously, although many an arrestee has blamed his arresting officers, he chose the illegal behavior with full knowledge of its potential consequences.

In the hilarious film, *Liar, Liar* (Universal, 1997), Jim Carrey plays a top-shelf defense attorney who is incapable of lying for one 24-hour period. When he's phoned by a career thug/client who's been locked up again and the fellow asks for legal advice, this distraught lawyer replies with uncharacteristic honesty, "Stop breaking the law, A-hole!!"

Couldn't we all do with such valuable legal advice? I don't mean we're all career thugs, but that we all (to some extent) go against what we know is right and then ask ourselves what went wrong. We all (to some extent) find ourselves from time to time on the wrong side of a friend, loved one, or complete stranger and begin casting about for *their* fault in the matter. *Applied smart power,* ASP, begins with the self.

Here's another way to put it: have you ever had a strong, negative reaction to a person's unacceptably negative behavior and later said that the person made you really angry? Well, if you're willing to blame another for "causing" anger in you, I'm sure you're also willing to acknowledge that you may, at some point, have "caused"

...we all (to some extent) go against what we know is right and then ask ourselves what went wrong.

**Extended to international relations,
these same principles can ease our
sometimes explosive clashes of cultures.**

---

the same. In other words, it follows that at some time during your life you have "made someone really angry."

Now look at the implication. He wasn't angry, then you did something, and then he became angry as a result. You *created* an angry person out of a not-angry one! You created the reality of having an angry person near you; you likewise created the reality of whatever consequences resulted. Did he yell at you? Did he kick you in the knee? Did he make fun of your car?

You created a negative event, whatever it was. If you had made some other choice instead, one that would not have "made" him angry, you wouldn't have had your feelings, knee, or pride hurt. You created your own hurt.

You may say, "Oh, yeah, that makes sense." You may ponder this idea and come to the conclusion that a little more mindfulness about our effect on others might go a long way—not necessarily for their benefit, but for our own! I believe being decent to others is in *my* best interests, regardless of the fact that it may improve the lives of others. If I happen to create happier or safer neighbors, well, that's just a bonus.

Powerful Peace, then, is a way for me to improve the world around me. Extended to international relations, these same principles can ease our sometimes explosive clashes of cultures.

On the other hand, if you think this is a load of hogwash and it makes you angry...please don't kick me in the knee.

INTO ACTION PLAN I

At the end of each section we'll capture a few of the referenced resources so you can look at the concepts from a fresh angle. These have helped form my ideas, and I hope they'll edify even while they entertain.

- Watch *Crash* and experience the complexity of good, bad, and culture clashes
- Watch *Hotel Rwanda* and try to comprehend the insanity of mutilating babies because of their ethnicity
- Read Nye, *The Future of Power*
- Watch *The Naked Gun* and try to hear the gangster's message in the bullets
- Read Covey, *Principle-Centered Leadership*
- Watch *John Q* and put yourself in his shoes
- Watch *Blackhawk Down* and watch the rescue efforts by Pakistani soldiers
- Watch *Liar, Liar* and watch for the negative consequences of lying, despite short-term gains

MIND

The Rational

Think Again

Breaking the cycle of harm is impossible without deliberate, *conscious* effort. The natural course of human conflict is to escalate until one side is defeated. If a fight is based on *misunderstanding*, every stab and kick means wasted energy. It's not only unnecessarily destructive, but discards energy that might be otherwise creative. Compounding this tragicomedy, such a fight drags both parties down to inferior positions in the end. Our Mind is the first human discriminator between basic, instinct-driven animal conduct and the higher capacity of our species.

**Not everyone can be a philosopher. But every
thinking person should reflect on the future and
meditate about the destiny of mankind here on earth.**
Mikhail Gorbachev

13 BALANCE
Kissing and killing

Smart power at the interpersonal level. That's what Powerful Peace advocates, but I wonder if the full message is coming through. It's called "smart" power, but it belongs to the visceral sense of humanity in Body, and especially to Heart and Soul, as well as to Mind. With the drawdown of U.S. operations for Operation Iraqi Freedom and my reintegration to American society following a recent year in Iraq, I sat down to take stock of the message so far—and how to say it going forward.

> **Our long-term security will come not from our ability to instill fear in other peoples, but through our capacity to speak to their hopes. And that work will best be done through the power of the decency and dignity of the American people —our troops and diplomats, but also our private sector, nongovernmental organizations and citizens. All of us have a role to play.**
> *Barack Obama*

My preoccupation with Iraq is a natural result of a military and civilian career involving that nation for many years. During the late 80's our eyes were glued to the Soviet threat. Even as Mikhail Gorbachev's *glasnost* and *perestroika* ("transparency" and "reconstruction") toppled the Cold War wall, Saddam Hussein's aggression

I snapped this while joking around with these kids through a base fence in Iraq. They had begged me for food. My heart breaks because we can't give them any, but my mind understands—if sharing at the fence becomes habitual, insurgents will strap an explosive suicide vest to a little child (again) and send him along with the rest.

against Kuwait drew the bulk of America's newly available attention. Iraq has been actively on our minds since the early 1990's.

With the September 11th attacks a decade later, the citizens of this planet entered a new era. My platoon helped "open the door" with reconnaissance operations, and U.S. military power flowed into Afghanistan in force. We conducted a dramatic reversal of Taliban influence there…then took our eyes off that ball and waded back into Iraq. In the absence of meaningful alternatives for the Afghan society, the Taliban reconstituted. As U.S. authorities in Iraq deliberated whether to leave earlier than planned, we found ourselves turning once more to unfinished business in Afghanistan and expecting several more years of determined combat. I headed back to Afghanistan.

If all this pinballing between wars in Iraq and Afghanistan seems to indicate a lack of effectiveness on our part, it's because, well, we hadn't been very effective. The proof is in the pudding. Don't get me wrong. I'm not criticizing the planners and implementers. I'm in no position to second-guess the decisions of good, highly experienced Coalition and policy leaders, armed with superior expertise and facing challenges of tremendous complexity. Nor, God forbid, am I saying the soldiers on the ground have not given their best. Remember—I am one. I'm simply pointing out the obvious. If we call a plumber to repair a leaky pipe, and the pipe continues to leak after he's paid and gone, he wasn't fully effective.

The pipes in Iraq and Afghanistan were still leaking. The good news is, we had learned to build a more effective team. No longer just an experienced fellow who knows how to swing a wrench…but *doesn't* understand how various metals corrode one another. We're bringing chemists for that. We're also bringing the water company, to determine whether the pressure is right. And a technician will walk through the house with us, demonstrating better ways to use the faucets so we can stress the pipes less…enough general contractor euphemisms for you?

Recent years in Iraq and Afghanistan have given the term "whole of government" acceptance as more than the feel-good jargon early critics assumed. Whole of government was officially mandated in the U.S. 2010 National Security Strategy. The introductory quote for this chapter is from President Barack Obama's foreword to that document.

We need to do a better job of kissing *and* killing. The military is expert at force, or hard power. And today we better understand that force alone provides—at best—only short-term gains, while setting the stage for possible long-term losses if it's overemphasized. As we add more kissing, or the soft power of influence, to include outreach and cultural awareness, we establish a better balance and better conditions for success. I emphasize *balance*—all too often, the message of smart power or "applied" smart power is misunderstood as merely an extension of soft power. Once again: without the underlying capacity for force, our soft persuasion can enjoy only limited effectiveness.

We need stable societies to carry on once force is removed. We need a smarter approach to societal engagement and development, a harmonized and holistic approach, so these populations can begin to support themselves and establish the foundation for enduring security. It will be interesting to see whether our future "repairs" turn out to be effective.

I emphasize *balance*—all too often, the message of smart power or "applied" smart power is misunderstood as merely an extension of soft power.

---

14 CONTEXT 1
On Rashids

The battlespace of conflict is littered with misunderstood motives, crossed cultures, intense self-interest and miscommunication. We will never change this universally, but wherever we change the field to any degree we increase security within the limits of our influence. Context provides that improved understanding.

Armageddon is not around the corner.
This is only what the people of violence want us to believe.
The complexity and diversity of the world is the hope for the future.
Michael Palin

Two of our Arab hosts from the opening chapter on September 11ᵗʰ both happened to be named Rashid. One, my friend, was the larger and more outgoing. "Little" Rashid, on the other hand, kept the American SEALs at arm's length, spending only as much time with our platoon as was necessary to complete the training we offered. You would rarely find Little Rashid sitting with Big Rashid and the rest of our motley international crew, laughing late into the evening over tea and a communal water pipe filled with sweet, dried fruit tobacco.

That evening of 9/11 was surreal in a once-in-a-lifetime way, of course. Both our groups were well informed in the intelligence of global terrorism. We all understood that the attackers were probably Arabs, probably connected to Osama bin Laden, and probably considered themselves good Muslims (though most of the hundreds of Muslims I have personally befriended around the world, in the

Clowning with Big Rashid in one another's "traditional" garb. We later watched side-by-side as the attacks of 9/11 unfolded. When the sun inevitably rose on September 12th, we weren't smiling like this.

years before and since 2001, adamantly disagree with al Qaeda's assertion that it represented all of Islam).

Arab and American SEALs sat silently through the tragedy together, until each one walked off to turn in for the night. No one had to articulate that with the next morning, our combat training exercises would be replaced by another kind of combat preparation. Last in the room to disengage from this world-changing event, I finally headed for my room to pack (once again) for war.

The next morning, little was said. We greeted one another, but there was no spirit for the typical banter and friendly abuses. Imagine instead a pack of wounded wolves, warily stalking around one another with an acute awareness of both private and shared pains.

When he caught sight of me in the compound, Big Rashid walked straight over. We both knew that the murderers had probably looked more like him than like me, and that they had probably grown up nearer to him than to me. We both also knew that we are friends, international and intercultural wars be damned. He looked me straight in the eye and said, "Rob—I'm sorry."

Little Rashid never said a word.

No one had to articulate that with the next morning, our combat training exercises would be replaced by another kind of combat preparation.

15

CONTEXT 2
On rapes

Knowledge is power. Whoever controls knowledge can control what we know, thus what we believe. Because we act based on what we believe, to some extent this influences what we do.

> **An ancient Sanskrit saying says, woman is the home and the home is the basis of society. If we build our homes, then we can build our country. If the home is inadequate…then that country cannot have harmony and no country which does not have harmony can grow in any direction at all. That is why women's education is almost more important than that of boys and men.**
> *Indira Gandhi*

While I was advising with the U.S. Special Forces in Iraq, one Operational Detachment, Alpha (ODA, or "A-Team") conducted the successful capture of an insurgent operative at his home. This mission went like clockwork. The operators entered the property, identified their target and detained the man with zero injury to the family and no shots fired.

As they were preparing to leave with the prisoner, his wife approached the team's interpreter. She had been as frightened as all wives and children are during these midnight raids, but had composed herself enough to tell this fellow Iraqi, "The foreign men [insurgent fighters from other towns and countries] told us that

> ...our adversaries (whether insurgent,
> terrorist, or dictator) are doing as well as
> or better in the Marketing competition.

whenever the American men come into houses to capture a man, they will always rape his wife. That didn't happen here."

As U.S. national military and civilian leadership are beginning to admit, our adversaries (whether insurgent, terrorist, or dictator) are doing as well as or better in the Marketing competition. The skill set known by the U.S. military as "Information Operations" (IO) is very effectively leveraged by some of our adversaries. (In subsequent chapters we'll look more at IO and other deliberate efforts to manipulate the beliefs and behaviors of individuals or groups.)

The interpreter passed her comment to the team leader, who was a quick-thinking young officer. Aware of the challenges we face in connecting with any skeptical, "occupied" population, and recognizing the tremendous value of having a trusted neighbor describe the whole truth of this raid, he directed the interpreter: "You tell this lady to go and say, to every woman she knows, everything she saw happen here tonight."

16 CONTEXT 3
On men of God

When we say, "Don't judge a book by its cover," we aren't usually speaking literally of books. More often, we're talking about another person. We're talking about the context of another person's life.

> **Every generation has the obligation to free men's minds for a look at new worlds, to look out from a higher plateau than the last generation. When I circled the moon and looked back at the Earth, my outlook on life and my viewpoint on Earth changed. By holding up my thumb at arm's length, I could completely blot out our planet. I suddenly realized how insignificant we are.**
> *James Lovell*

Appearances can be deceiving.

One of my best friends from my most recent year in Iraq is a mature, devout Muslim from Egypt named Kamy. Superficially, you could easily compare Kamy to the late Osama bin Laden's Egyptian partner and subsequent leader of al Qaeda, Ayman al-Zawahiri. His national background is similar, the devotional mark on his forehead (from pressing it to the floor during prayer) is similar, his beard is similar and even his eyes are similar. They could pass for brothers. Where Kamy clearly differs from Ayman, however, is in a phrase I was moved to hear him say: "God bless America!"

The American story of racial conflicts is thoroughly saturated with fears and ignorance on all sides.

If you think it unlikely that a leader of AQ would utter the same, you're probably right. On the other hand, the United States was scandalized during one presidential campaign to hear an American Christian preacher shout: "God *damn* America!"

You will have your own opinion about that infamous sound bite which posed such a challenge for the Obama campaign. Very likely you fall into one of two camps: the one that thinks nothing could justify such an outrageous comment, or the one that understands his motivation (remember the phrase *empathize with?*) As for me, I hear a lifetime's frustration and hurt in the angry outburst from Reverend Jeremiah Wright. I imagine a chronic sense of societal marginalization, among the most painful experiences a man of any race, religion or nationality can suffer. I hear a stinging resentment built up over many years of perceived injustices. None of this means I appreciate his comment; only that I think I can begin to comprehend its origin.

Notice also that I wrote "perceived injustices." This does not imply that his grievances are either real or unfounded; only that he perceives them strongly. Some are probably inaccurate to a degree, through the action of his own filters or the agenda of others who taught him. Again, one common root of conflict is misunderstanding. The American story of racial conflicts is thoroughly saturated with fears and ignorance on all sides. In an ironic and all-too-common twist, the resentment-driven, melodramatic outburst of "God damn America!" by a black American minister further inflamed resentment among select white circles (some of whom are always looking out for reasons to criticize African-Americans), and worsened the general experience of some other blacks in America.

17

CONTEXT 4
Inside out and upside down

We've looked into some faces from the universe of conflict. Now let's try to look out from those same faces.

Perhaps travel cannot prevent bigotry, but by demonstrating that all peoples cry, laugh, eat, worry, and die, it can introduce the idea that if we try and understand each other, we may even become friends.
Maya Angelou

Think about Little Rashid, the insurgent's wife, and Kamy for a moment. What lay behind these events? More importantly, what might lie ahead? A little mindfulness goes a long way.

Why didn't Little Rashid express sympathy for his American counterparts following 9/11? Why did the young Special Forces leader insist that the wife tell other women everything that had happened? Why did Egyptian Kamy blurt out, "God bless America!" with tears in his eyes?

We need to bring an end to two-dimensional thinking where breath and blood and families are on the line. We are not a two-dimensional species. Our loves and

---

We need to bring an end to two-dimensional thinking where breath and blood and families are on the line.

66

Our loves and hates are of
an equal opportunity nature.

hates are of an equal opportunity nature. People as unlike as a pious Egyptian Muslim and a provocative American Christian preacher can take completely unexpected, opposite stances…based on each one's unique set of life experiences.

Context is crucial to Powerful Peace. Motives matter. It's very important to consider a person's point of view.

I speculate that Little Rashid was conflicted in his feelings about the 9/11 attacks. Millions more around the world were also torn—between revulsion at the devastation on one hand, and the "comeuppance" they thought the U.S. had long deserved. To find an American analogy for context, we only have to consider World War II American feelings about the approximately one quarter million civilian deaths inflicted by the bombings at Hiroshima and Nagasaki. The prevailing U.S. mood was one of grim righteousness, even though a quarter million immolated civilians is in no way proportionate to the 3,000 professional military men killed on the Day of Infamy.

In contrast, deliberate misinformation can also lead to dangerous misunderstanding. The wife of the captured insurgent, the lady who feared being violated according to a fictitious U.S. policy of institutional rape, highlighted a serious problem of perception. The young Special Forces team leader demonstrated its solution. The enemy had managed to convince at least one isolated population that American soldiers will always brutalize a detainee's wife. It's brilliant. Consider how this might compel even an innocent man to fight to the death as an unwitting pawn. Believing his family to be at risk as a consequence of his own arrest, he can be co-opted as an unwitting weapon for the insurgency.

Finally, consider immediate conditions at the moment of an unexpected occurrence. We've explored Reverend Wright's motivation for his outrageous comment, but what about Kamy's spontaneous praise of America? I had just pointed out a young Iraqi boy on our base who had been flown round-trip with his father, courtesy of Uncle Sam, for a lifesaving surgery in Europe. It's common for Special Forces commanders to allocate funds this way. The child's operation was an investment in that local society…and in the security of the United States. One small boy, one deeply grateful family, and one neighborhood were all changed for the better—and they will always remember the source of their minor miracle.

Kamy and I would sometimes sit and talk in the evenings, he serenely puffing his pipe and I my cigar, respectfully discussing matters of differing faiths, matters of war, of suffering, and of respect itself. We are very different in very many ways, but it was easy to find common ground; we are commonly humans.

An IO officer friend told me his department's goal is to be "first to the truth" in reaching a local population. Truth is a cornerstone of Powerful Peace.

Powerful Peace is *not* a handy eight-step program for being a safer or nicer person. It is just our best effort to find the truth on origins of conflict, shown through examples of fighting and, more importantly, alternatives to fighting. Our story has a lot of violence, because that's the reality of our world. It's because of the violence that we have to discuss conflict management at all.

Opening one's mind to consider the *context* of an apparent conflict is one of the easiest ways to begin defusing its destructive potential.

18 CONSCIOUS BIGOTRY
A big T for tolerance

Most bias against complete strangers on the basis of race, religion, etc. is not at all funny. Most such bigotry is disgusting, exasperating to outsiders, and very, very difficult to justify through frank and mature dialogue. Thank goodness we have ridiculous examples like the following to make the problem easier to examine.

Look back, to slavery, to suffrage, to integration and one thing is clear. Fashions in bigotry come and go. The right thing lasts.
Anna Quindlen

Every once in a while I stop racing around for a few minutes and watch something on TV. Maybe it's a rerun of Monk, or another sophisticated treat, Frasier. My all-time favorite comedy series, though, has got to be Comedy Central's Reno 911.

If you've never experienced "Lieutenant Jim Dangle" in his "law enforcement cheetah" uniform short-shorts and the rest of the radically flawed, fictitious cops of the Reno Sheriff's Department, you are missing out. They pursue radically flawed criminals and attempt to mete out a double helping of justice, Reno-style.

We'll return to *Reno 911* in a bit.

Intolerance and bigotry can be more destructive to the *holder's* well-being and quality of life than those of his victims.

Take religion, for example. After decades in global security and service in 30-plus nations at various stages of peace and war, I've seen some countries that

With commando friend Salim, whose name means "peace." Salim doesn't look like me; doesn't dress like me… yet he has chosen to step forward and stand in the gap like any warrior, anywhere the world.

don't share America's cherished belief in personal freedom. The Maldives comes to mind. Citizens of the Republic of Maldives are Muslims. Period. That's what the government says, and they get to make the call. I guess it helps cut down on census questions or something.

Many Americans today say that the United States is a Christian nation. I suppose that's originally, technically true, since most of the Founding Fathers were more or less Christians with some secular humanism mixed in. We should keep in mind, however, that these heroes of the American experiment in human freedom are the same great leaders who hammered out and fought over rules forbidding the forbidding of other religions, or the establishment of any one state religion… for both their generation, and our own.

This is an excellent example of institutionalized tolerance. I ask you: how brilliant were these first patriots, who could foresee and forestall problems that would perplex us and bring us to blows a quarter of a millennium later? They didn't even have Google!

Take also the freedoms to assemble, to speak, and to publish. I've written that Americans are better than our fears. We're bigger than our suspicions. We must remain close to those ideals that first breathed life into the *United* States of America, and leave that lamp burning before Americans—and America admirers—for many generations to come. We owe this to our ancestors of 1776…and our descendants of 2276.

Intolerance and bigotry can be more destructive to the holder's well-being and quality of life than those of his victims.

> Since bigotry can be so obviously deliberate,
> it's reassuring to remember the earliest
> Americans as equally deliberate, locking in
> place a system for institutionalized tolerance.

Okay, that's it for the dramatic sweep of history bit. Back to our *Reno 911* absurdity. One of my most favorite episodes involves a public disturbance call to a house where KKK members Gary and Lyle are standing in white robes beside a large wooden cross. A third Klansman is holding a torch.

Jones, the stereotypical black deputy (don't worry—everybody in this show is stereotyped, and to wondrous effect), says Ah, Hell No and pulls out his pistol. "You're lighting a damn cross in your own yard??"

Gary responds, "Oh, see, that's not a cross. That's a T…for Tolerance. It's a T for Truth." Now, with his voice breaking in the intensity of his apparent newfound love for people of all races, he continues, "It's a T for Turning the corner." Addressing his friends, he shouts, "Fire it up!"

Jones cocks his pistol and says, "I'll f'ing light *you* up!"

Gary replies to Jonesy, "You know, I'm getting a lot of hostility from you. That's a T. It's a T for Team because I understand it now. Now we're all on a Team."

In the ensuing fracas, as Gary tries to give Jones a big hug, the torchbearer inadvertently ignites Lyle's robes but leaves the T unscorched. While they all watch Lyle run around in flames, Gary comments, "You know, he's accident prone. This is not a complete surprise."

Since bigotry can be so obviously deliberate, it's reassuring to remember the earliest Americans as equally deliberate, locking in place a system for institutionalized tolerance. It may never be possible to bring all people into a mental pattern of mutual respect for diversity and cultures, but such systems at least provide the structure to let it happen where it may.

19 UNCONSCIOUS BIGOTRY
Fed poison

Bigotry is not always as plain as the desire to ignite a big wooden T. The bias you and I carry is a subconscious product of experiences, too. I may admire a politician and fail to acknowledge widespread claims of his blatant corruption, simply because he once made a positive impression. I may never discover the pleasure and health benefits of eating apples, if as a young child I nearly choked to death on one and carry an irrational aversion. Many unconscious motivators drive our behavior.

There really is a palpable moral component to our beings and it can be contaminated. Moral contamination almost never announces itself; it is always a very small, seemingly silent, inconsequential event, but it is like radiation; it accumulates, and there are no permissible safe levels.
E. B. Doctorow

I need to confess something: my brain doesn't always think the way I wish it would. Sometimes ideas streak through which embarrass, disappoint, and even shame me. There's an occasional inconsistency between my high ideals of balanced peacemaking through increased understanding…and the real world of daily thinking.

I was once driving downtown on a bright and summery day. My parents were flying in for our first reunion in years. It came as quite a surprise to suddenly find myself entertaining disrespectful, racist thoughts.

I've come to believe that destructive ideas are very real objects that can reproduce and multiply in fertile minds, popping up later and causing further harm...

It didn't start out to be a racist day. To be fair, it wasn't really a racist day at all. This event was merely a moment, a brief thought that flickered and was gone, leaving me mentally scratching my figurative head and blinking in surprise at myself.

Cruising along, I had been admiring God's work in numerous little details: clear sky; centuries of architecture; the priceless legacy of one of America's most historic cities. Suddenly, when I passed two human beings who don't look like me, a derogatory term flashed to mind.

I won't tell you what that term was. This isn't because I fear to be labeled an actual racist, but because I've come to believe that destructive ideas are very real objects that can reproduce and multiply in fertile minds, popping up later and causing further harm—like thistles, or venomous spiders. I won't be responsible for breeding more.

If I carelessly warn you to "watch out!" for a certain individual, for example, you may take my words to heart and be on your guard with him. It doesn't matter that this third person may be a wonderful human being, and my information flawed. Your opinion is now stained. Whatever mutual benefit you may have one day enjoyed with that person, the potential is degraded because a negative seed got into your head and took root.

Children are the ultimate intellectual fertile ground. They believe what they're told because they have no choice, no baseline, to say otherwise. In all the places and situations that are brand new for them, their trusted guardians have the only history available.

Consider the aforementioned Ku Klux Klan, or other terrorist groups. Adult mentors may dress a toddler up in white robes or a mock suicide vest. To gain the approval of his adult mentors, he'll parade around "hating" blacks or Jews, according to the organization's teachings. I would argue that he can't even understand what it really means to hate...yet. But he will. Practice anything, and you'll get good at it.

Does this mean I was taught to hate by my parents, or that I teach my own children the same? Absolutely not. In fact, I would rate my family of origin as being more tolerant than most. Our day-to-day environment, however, stealthily insinuates unwelcome thoughts like poison. They aren't easily recognized when ingested. The racial slur that popped into my mind is not one I've ever deliberately spoken—yet it leapt up like any other thought when triggered, as would the term "punch buggy" if you noticed a Volkswagen Bug.

I have to raise a final example about toxic words carelessly scattered: in some pop circles today, the verb "pimp" is very casually applied to mean the fun upgrading of some object—a car (pimp my ride), a home (pimp my crib), or some other *thing*. Let us not forget the word's origin. A *noun* pimp is a man who, in effect, owns human things. Typically, the human things he owns are women. He is a modern-day slaveholder. It's become popularly amusing to speak of the "Pimp Slap," or joke around the office, "Bitch, where's my money?" Yet we understand that to maintain control of his property, fellow humans, the pimp may in fact degrade and abuse, verbally and physically. He may hook his things on addictive drugs, severing their freedom to run away. Under some circumstances, he even kills.

I'll take this uncomfortable discussion one step further and refer to Nicholas Kristof and Sheryl WuDunn's amazing book, *Half the Sky; Turning Oppression into Opportunity for Women Worldwide* (Alfred A. Knopf, 2009). I can't recommend this work strongly enough. (You'll read more about this topic in chapter 44.)

I told you up front I was going to point at some elephants. The detestable word "pimp" is one of the least challenged, most foul expressions in common English use. It deserves our utter contempt, not popularization. One of the examples given by Kristof and WuDunn concerns a 15-year-old Cambodian girl named Srey Rath on her first realizing she had been sold into sexual slavery in Malaysia:

> "She fought back, enraging the customer. 'So the boss got angry and hit me in the face, first with one hand and then the other,' she remembers, telling her story with simple resignation. 'The mark stayed on my face for two weeks.' Then the boss and the other gangsters raped her and beat her with their fists.

A pimp is a man who, in effect, owns human things. Typically, the human things he owns are women. He is a modern-day slaveholder.

Let's continue to examine our assumptions and resist the casual spread of symbols of involuntary hatred.

"'You have to serve the customers,' the boss told her as he punched her. 'If not, we will beat you to death. Do you want that?'

"The girls were forced to work in the brothel seven days a week, fifteen hours a day. They were kept naked to make it more difficult for them to run away or to keep tips or other money, and they were forbidden to ask customers to use condoms. They were battered until they smiled constantly and simulated joy at the sight of customers, because men would not pay as much for sex with girls with reddened eyes and haggard faces."

Srey managed to escape after some time, making her way with some other sex slaves to a local police station:

"The police first tried to shoo them away, then arrested the girls for illegal immigration. Rath served a year in prison under Malaysia's tough anti-immigrant laws, and then she was supposed to be repatriated. She thought a Malaysian policeman was escorting her home when he drove her to the Thai border—but then he sold her to a trafficker, who peddled her to a Thai brothel."

Think about Srey the next time you consider using the word "pimp" casually. It is fundamentally identical to the early American institution of slavery. In recent decades, our nation staggered through a bloody, final, official liberation of ourselves *from ourselves* and that despicable, persistent spawn of slavery, segregation. Great men and women were led by that titan of unbreakable courage, Dr. Martin Luther King, Jr. They unflinchingly put their heads under heavy wooden clubs, swung by agents of a nation riddled with the diseases of fear and hatred. They were compelled by a dream that one day no man would be called a nigger—by anyone of any race. And they did it so no woman would be enslaved, brutalized, and possibly killed—as a whore.

I hope you will remember that words carry tremendous power. Let's continue to examine our assumptions and resist the casual spread of symbols of involuntary hatred. Let's share words mindfully, and refuse to sow poisonous ones. In our daily microcosm, let us be mindful that poisonous words breed poisonous thoughts and actions that contaminate the macrocosm we all share.

20 PRIDE
Don't be a roadblock

In Iraq, where I've spent much of my recent life, people are really dying. Ditto for Afghanistan and other crisis areas. They're dying as a direct result of the fighting going on in a struggle for supremacy between various factions. Some of those dying, still, are innocent children. The tragedy is made worse when such deaths result from ego struggles.

If it's true that our species is alone in the universe, then I'd have to say the universe aimed rather low and settled for very little.
George Carlin

I like to believe that not much upsets my applecart. I usually try to look at differing viewpoints as learning opportunities. One theme of Powerful Peace is that no one among us knows everything; thus every one of us can teach every one of us something.

Where my high-falutin' ideals break down, however, is in the realm of ego and flexing petty authority…under life-and-death conditions. In theory, each of us involved in prosecuting—and concluding—these conflicts is on the same team and shares a sense of urgency toward our responsibility of working for security. In theory.

Contrast such a shared urgency, and its corresponding willingness to cooperate / compromise where necessary, with the motivation of a petty tyrant. This person may be in a position of some great authority, or just a little. Typically, the petty tyrant

This is not a dump zone.

Use the green bin around the corner.

You lazy bastards

I spent some months as a liaison officer to the British forces in Basra, Iraq. One thing's certain: my UK mates won't mind this sign being used as an example of "pride." They're rightly proud of their talent for comical abuse!

is not an actual commander, but a pretender who thinks his obstructive behavior is commander-ly. Alexander Pushkin wrote of this dynamic in his classic, *The Station Master*: "Who has not hated the station masters? Who has not quarreled with them?"

I was roadblocked in Iraq by a petty tyrant who called to inform my team he would not be "authorizing" a particular piece of infrastructure we required. I could almost envision him, behind the safety of the telephone line, puffing up his chest at the other end like a little rooster. This petty tyrant, little more than a clerk in a high-ranking uniform, was getting off on denying us something.

Flash forward to potential outcomes. That piece of infrastructure (communications, power or transportation, for example) is required by a team (special operations, information technology or logistics) to complete its mission. A petty tyrant successfully denies its issuance. The mission (a raid, satellite dish installation or food delivery) is not accomplished. The mission fails. The denial of basic functionality is basically a casualty of some punk's desire to raise himself and feel important through the mechanism of reducing someone else. As a result, mission readiness is diminished.

I was roadblocked in Iraq by a petty tyrant who called to inform my team he would not be "authorizing" a particular piece of infrastructure we required.

It isn't hard to think through potential
negative consequences, but it does seem
difficult for many of us to just humble-down
a little and try to get along with others.

To take the analogy a little farther, think through this denial that causes a raid to be aborted.

Imagine that a Bad Man who would have been captured by a successful raid is left to operate freely for a few more weeks. During that time he executes a VBIED (vehicle-borne improvised explosive device, or car bomb) attack against a police station. Seven dead daddies never go home to their families. One dead commander never leads a crucial overhaul of a corrupt security force. One neighborhood is left undefended, and many more die in the chaos during the year it takes to rebuild that station.

It isn't hard to think through potential negative consequences, but it does seem difficult for many of us to just humble-down a little and try to get along with others. Shame on us.

21 ARROGANCE
The six blind wise men and the elephant

Our species' remarkable talent for brilliant idiocy and violent disagreement has been recorded for millennia. This paraphrasing of an ancient parable paints an elegant picture. I love this story—it has probably been retold with thousands of variations over thousands of years, with the number of wise men varying and any assortment of misconceived items depending on what might be indigenous to local tellers. Needless to say, the details are not important. In fact, for those of us who secretly desire for there to be "just one way" to tell it, we're probably acting out the nature of blind wise men in real time!

O how they cling and wrangle, some who claim
For preacher and monk the honored name!
For, quarreling, each to his view they cling.
Such folk see only one side of a thing.
The Buddha

Once there were six wise men who were blind. They walked everywhere together and talked about very wise things, each outdoing the next with his great wisdom.

On one particularly pleasant spring day, the six blind wise men were walking on the road, discussing very wise things and outdoing one another with their great wisdom. They came upon an elephant and its handler, resting on the way.

I love this sign. Yes, it may have been overly optimistic to believe hanging around nearby would protect me from car bombs, but hey; I had to hang around somewhere!

The six blind wise men had never before "seen" an elephant, although they had heard of such from travelers. Each approached to touch the beast and better understand this marvelous creature.

The first approached near the head and, tracing his hands all around the elephant's trunk, confidently announced to his friends that an elephant is definitely like a python.

The second, near the first, laid his hands upon the tusk and declared the first mistaken; an elephant is like a spear.

The third touched the animal's flapping ear and said these two were fools. An elephant is like a fan.

Next was a leg (which proved an elephant is like a tree) and the flank (obviously, an elephant is like a wall).

Finally, all the way 'round the farthest, otherest end, the last wise man held the tail in his hands and laughed at the folly of all his friends. It was plain that an elephant is like a rope. Soon the disagreement turned into a shouted argument, as each pressed harder to prove his version of the truth. Next they fell to blows.

The dull-witted but kindly elephant handler shook his head in wonder at all the violent wisdom tumbling around on the ground and continued on his way with the great beast—which he could clearly see was not any one of the things they said, but all and more.

These six blind wise men were very learned and very honest. Not one held deception in his heart, yet they described wildly different realities and fought one another in their pride of certainty. Much has changed but nothing has changed since the day the six blind wise men discovered the elephant…except that there are more than *seven billion* of us blind, wise men today.

Each one of us has a limited worldview, and it takes courage to acknowledge that and act accordingly.

Each one of us has a limited worldview, and it takes courage to acknowledge that and act accordingly. My small human nature urges me to defend my ignorance with all my strength.

Although I am a Christian, I don't claim that as a blank check to make smug, blanket statements about other ways of life. In fact, I have a special request for my Christian friends (we'll use us as the example): if you haven't learned about other faiths as expressed *from their faithful*, please don't scatter second-hand stories of judgment like supermarket tabloids. It isn't Christ-like.

One of my preachers, years ago, declared that before Jesus came, the world had never known compassion. Unfortunately, he dug himself in deeper and specifically mentioned the Buddha, and how the Buddha had never taught compassion. This preacher friend of mine had never studied the faith personally; he'd merely heard about it, and that was from other unfriendly sources. I, on the other hand, had studied Buddhism—and even practiced it years earlier.

In one of the earliest stories about the boy who would come to be known as the Buddha, he observed a worm turned up by a farmer's spade in a field. A bird flew down and snatched up this worm to eat it. The little boy, a prince, was deeply saddened by the suffering of even so lowly a creature as the worm. He was moved by compassion.

Another all-too-common trend among some Christian teachers these days is to make sweeping statements of condemnation about Islam. Again, they often haven't actually examined the faith *with interpretation* from Muslims, but have willingly accepted sometimes outlandish stories from its harshest critics. As with Buddhism, I have examined Islam personally...and discussed it with hundreds of practicing Muslim friends, in at least a dozen predominantly-Muslim nations.

Outright condemnation will put any group on the defensive. If there is a general assault on Islam, some among that group will react defensively. Thus begins, or continues, an escalation.

Please hear my heart, Christian brethren: I am most definitely not holier than thou. In fact, I've often said that if Paul called himself Chief Among Sinners, I suppose I'd have to be his Deputy Chief. What I'm saying to Christ-followers,

> **Whether we're looking at gender, racial, political, financial or other issues, it's helpful to look at ourselves and at the world through our adversary's eyes.**

others-followers, and no-one-followers is that, despite our intense ego urgings to declare final victory over the mysteries that so confound us all, sometimes we'll just have to have to accept a draw and respect that others see the world differently. If you believe in God, you probably recognize that any eternal God worth the title must, by definition, be greater than the capacity of our little human thoughts and words to contain. In other words, not any one of us can have it exactly right.

It would behoove us all, therefore, to imitate God…and give a little grace to our fellows down here.

This chapter is on arrogance and "blindness," of course, and not religion. It certainly isn't meant to be a Christian-bashing. Sadly, the practice of any religion often provides plenty of material for a case study on the destructive quality of arrogance. Whether we're looking at gender, racial, political, financial or other issues, it's helpful to look at ourselves and at the world through our adversary's eyes. We just might notice a plank in our own.

22 IGNORANCE
When complexion kills

Bigots are everywhere. I'm sure we're all prejudiced to some extent...I also suspect that most of us underestimate our own level of prejudice.

**Education is not simply about academic achievement.
As spelled out in the Universal Declaration of Human Rights,
it is about understanding, tolerance, and friendship,
which are the basis of peace in our world.**
Aung San Suu Kyi

My white, Christian, American friend Bill was in an Arab Muslim country a few years ago when a particularly destructive U.S. attack killed a large number of innocent civilians. Until this tragedy, Bill had a great job as a manager with a local company. When following this attack he was told that his position was being eliminated for company right-sizing, he was stunned.

Bill was shouted at and threatened by local citizens, complete strangers, who took out their anger on him personally for a tragedy over which he had had no control.

Later he discovered that he, the only American and the only Christian, had also been the only casualty of this so-called "right-sizing."

After the attack, Bill was shouted at and threatened by local citizens, complete strangers, who took out their anger on him personally for a tragedy over which he had had no control. He was even spit upon, and he felt totally helpless to seek support from the local authorities.

Bill told me that even non-Americans were assaulted because of this blind rage. In a few rare cases, they were murdered. A Canadian Jew was killed in his own shop, because a rampaging hothead couldn't distinguish between the American "Crusaders" who had conducted the original military strike and some who happened to look like them.

My friend Andy, who lives in that same Muslim country, tells me the bigotry is so pervasive he has a wry term to describe his position: the Caucasian Christian Cat, or 3C. He tells me that the 3C is by far the worst "type" to be these days. He's guilty until proven innocent, and he's distrusted on sight. It's a very uncomfortable feeling. There's nothing he can do about it.

Ironically, Andy is a citizen of that country. He was born there. He just doesn't "look" right.

If you're like me, this makes your blood boil. It's outrageous that decent, law-abiding, good "Christian Americans" like Bill and Andy can be treated so unfairly. They never hurt anyone. They should get the same respect the locals give each other in that country...you probably agree, right?

Good. And now I'll admit: I've been a little deceptive in this account so far.

My friend Bill is not originally an American. He's not a Christian, either.

He's also not named Bill. His name is Bassam.

The "attack" which killed so many innocent civilians was not an American one, but Islamic-extremist. It was conducted by Arabs. It was against the Twin Towers and the Pentagon on September 11, 2001.

Bassam is a retired Jordanian Army officer and a naturalized citizen of the United States. Soon after 9/11 this Arab Muslim was fired by a major retailer in America; before the attacks he had received regular praise for his excellence in management. After 9/11, the "right size" for that firm appears to have meant one less Arab Muslim.

Bassam was spit upon, but not in some faraway land. He was spit upon by a fellow American because he looks like some of the people who carried out 9/11. He was deeply hurt by these humiliating abuses, but even more so because he loves his adopted country very much. He, like so many others, wanted only to grieve with his American family. Instead he was treated like an enemy.

The murdered Canadian Jew is also not as I described. He was an Indian Sikh. He was murdered in America, shot to death by an American in a deliberate act of vengeance, four days after September 11th. He was murdered because he wore a turban. According to family members, this non-Muslim South Asian had been deeply distraught over the suffering in America caused by 9/11.

Finally, Andy's actual name is Imran. He was born an American and raised by American parents. They share the ethnic features common to Pakistan.

Andy—Imran—did *not* tell me he's a 3C. It's actually 3M. The "hardest type to be in America," according to Imran and many of my other friends, is a Middle-Eastern, Muslim Male. Ironically, these are the same individuals who could best identify and reach into the source of hate that led to the attacks. Deliberately engaging guys like Imran, instead of rejecting and antagonizing them, would be a really good way to start discovering solutions.

23 UNDERSTANDING
Cultural Blindness

The story of Powerful Peace in one word is "understanding." With understanding we can recognize sources of conflict in advance and prevent hostility, once we've developed the right message. If necessary, understanding of the enemy helps us defeat him. There's just no downside to understanding more.

**I don't think we understood the cultural,
historic influences that pushed them into that position.
It might have helped us ward the whole thing off
if we had understood the deeper currents in the situation.**
Stansfield Turner

Stansfield Turner ran the Central Intelligence Agency during the Carter administration. In the above quote from 1995, he was reflecting on the 1979 Soviet invasion of Afghanistan. *Invisible History—Afghanistan's Untold Story* (City Lights Publishers, 2009) clarifies the mind-boggling complexity of Afghanistan's internal and external influences during the century and a half up to and including the ten-year long Soviet adventure. It resulted in tremendous suffering and loss for many, and contributed to the collapse of the Soviet Union.

I've conducted multiple assignments in Afghanistan. Anticipating several more years' traveling into and out of this troubled nation, I've been studying the circumstances that led to today's mess.

1991. Best Turkish friend Hayri prepares to correct me for yet another shockingly offensive, inadvertent mutilation of his language.

Cultural awareness is not some nice-to-have component in effective strategic and policy planning. It's an essential piece. It's a literal do-or-die piece. We should constantly seek to understand other ways of life, because today it is a matter of life or death.

That 1979 Afghan invasion ended in a humbling withdrawal. The Soviets met the same fate as every invader since Alexander the Great. Their experience in this case is frequently compared to the American experience in Vietnam.

I'd like to provide a more personal and recognizable anecdote from my own past to demonstrate the dangerous absurdity of misunderstanding:

Ali was a Turkish friend of mine during a year's assignment to a remote base in his country. We enjoyed spending weekends downing Efes beer and shish kebab at our restaurant hangout down by the beach. One fateful night, however, he surprised me with an outburst of violent hostility. Looking back, I know that with a *much* deeper contextual understanding I could have seen it coming and, as Director Turner said, "warded it off."

There was a Dutch tourist staying in our little coastal town, and it was no secret Ali also had his eye on her. When I finally finagled a dinner date for one Saturday night, I naturally felt like the winner of the Rob vs. Ali competition for female attention. It was probably a mistake to arrange that dinner date for the same club where he and I normally partied....

Cultural awareness is not some nice-to-have component in effective strategic and policy planning. It's an essential piece. It's a literal do-or-die piece.

While she and I snacked on feta cheese and olives, I made clumsy small talk and turned the discussion—ridiculously—to astrology (as in, "what's your sign?") Unfortunately, this European had only a partial grasp of English, and I knew only two phrases in Dutch. Considering the newness of our acquaintance, neither was yet appropriate.

The word "astrology" failed to clear it up, as did "zodiac." When I said I'm a Taurus, she only stared blankly. The word "bull" fell flat next. I realized my attempt at a clever joke was rapidly careening off a social cliff. It was time for date-saving physical gestures.

Extending both index fingers, I placed them alongside my temples to depict a boy cow's horns. That's when all Turkish hell broke loose.

Within seconds, Ali had charged up and struck me in the shoulder. I hadn't even known he was at the club that night! He shouted, "Did you do this to me???" in some sort of Turkenglish and placed his fingers at his own temples. Four more ticked-off Turks (it's best to be *behind* ticked-off Turks, and not in front) glared at me over his shoulder.

I was utterly flabbergasted. My date was frightened. In broken Turkish, I told him plainly that I didn't know what the blank he was talking about. This only seemed to aggravate him further, but the whole unpleasant mess eventually resolved without becoming more physical. After a couple of tense minutes, Ali and his posse stalked away. The dinner was ruined.

I had planned to sleep on the beach that evening. Needless to say, this ended up being a one-eye-open, sleepless night. Angry Turkish knives can slice tent fabric as easily as a throat.

When I raised the matter with best friend Hayri the next day, he was aghast. As if explaining a "grown-up" topic to a dimwitted child (that's me), he finally managed to convey that, colloquially, the Turkish word "to gore" (*boynuzlemek*) means "to cheat on your man." In other words, if a fellow isn't "man enough" (if you know what I mean) to keep a woman happy, she will go off with another, *better* man. She leaves the first "gored."

Already stewing and angry at me for "getting the girl," Ali had now thought I was joking about his being unmanly! Still worse, for his fully developed Turkish machismo and my immediate safety, he believed a *woman* had been laughing at a joke about his being…inadequate…in the man department. I'm lucky to be alive!

Of course, that evening's potential for me to receive an ass whupping is negligible, when compared to the immeasurable pain endured during the 1980's

---

Contrary to the machismo in my own American
culture, "being understanding" is not a form of
weakness. Knowledge is in fact, power.

---

fiasco in Afghanistan, but the value of preventing/clearing up misunderstanding is fundamentally the same. We would have been more effective in Afghanistan—and I would have been on that date—through deeper cultural comprehension. Contrary to the machismo in my own American culture, "being understanding" is not a form of weakness. Knowledge is in fact, power. You will make your life better by considering the power of your impact on others.

PS: Be very careful with those hand gestures.

24 CHANGE
"A tremendous responsibility to humanity"

Improving our approach to national and international security is a non-partisan—I prefer "apolitical"—undertaking. In this chapter I'll pull references from both sides of the aisle and, at the end, a completely aisle-free source: one of my own, earliest writings on balanced peacemaking.

In the last seven years, we have spent the treasure of our nation —young American soldiers, first and foremost, and billions of dollars— to fight terrorism, and yet grave questions remain as to whether or not we have chosen our battles correctly.
John Kerry

The opening quote was recorded during Hillary Rodham Clinton's Secretary of State Confirmation Hearing, taken from *Democratic* Senator John Kerry's introductory comments. He continued, "Pakistan and Afghanistan are definitively the front line.... It is clear that no amount of additional troops will succeed absent the effective instruments of a functioning state...I believe we must fundamentally redefine our approach."

...We must fundamentally redefine our approach.

Republican Senator Richard Lugar, an active supporter of the U.S. Institute of Peace, was quoted in the same hearing: "The United States cannot feed every person…or stop every conflict, but our power and status have conferred upon us a tremendous responsibility to humanity."

…Our power and status have conferred upon us a tremendous responsibility to humanity.

In her own comments at the confirmation hearing, *Democratic* Senator Clinton praised Secretary of Defense Robert Gates—the same Bob Gates who had been appointed by *Republican* President George W. Bush: "Secretary Gates… has been particularly eloquent in articulating the importance of diplomacy…. As he has stated, 'Our civilian institutions of diplomacy and development have been chronically undermanned and underfunded for far too long.'"

Let's contrast this expressed intent for inter-departmental cooperation with the following ominous message from *World at Risk: The Report of the Commission on the Prevention of WMD Proliferation and Terrorism,* (Vintage Books, 2008): "Unless the world community acts decisively and with great urgency, it is more likely than not that a weapon of mass destruction will be used in a terrorist attack somewhere in the world by the end of 2013."

The new Secretary of State also said:

> "We must use what has been called smart power, the full range of tools at our disposal—diplomatic, economic, military, political, legal, and cultural—picking the right tool or combination of tools for each situation. With smart power, diplomacy will be the vanguard of our foreign policy…even when we cannot fully agree with some governments we share a bond of humanity with their people…. *Investing in our common humanity through social development is not marginal to our foreign policy but essential to the realization of our goals….* More than two billion people worldwide live on less than $2 a day…. Our pleas will fall on deaf ears unless democracy actually improves people's lives…." [Italics mine.]

Investing in our common humanity through social development is not marginal to our foreign policy but essential to the realization of our goals…

In summary, we are seeing a flood of fresh, bipartisan attention to smart power, and an urgent need to support unstable populations and engage diplomatically as one means of countering terrorism and violent conflict.

In light of Secretary Clinton's 2009 comments on smart power, please review the following shameless plug from an essay I wrote for a U.S. agency in 2005:

"What is crucial is a case-by-case use of the most effective methods for each problem. Some crises of hostility can be resolved with dialogue to reduce misunderstanding; some, for now, still demand a 'kinetic solution' from the business end of a rifle.... Best of all, however, will be the next evolution of threat mitigation: elimination, before the hateful cause exists, by working with the source.... If we care to understand well enough, open exchange and cooperation can starve the very roots of terrorism. Statecraft and interpersonal engagement are more important, in the long run, than military might."

That's *applied* smart power, written *four years* before Secretary Clinton's public pronouncement on smart power. Why don't we citizens continue to lead from the bottom, with Powerful Peace and an active PeaceHawks.org network? Eventually, our efforts and those of the policy makers can meet in the middle for the benefit of humanity.

INTO ACTION PLAN II

- Watch *Reno 911...* But check your self-righteousness at the door so you can enjoy it!
- Read Kristof and WuDunn, *Half the Sky; Turning Oppression into Opportunity for Women Worldwide*
- Read Fitzgerald and Gould, *Invisible History*
- Read the "WMD Commission's" *World at Risk*

SECTION III

HEART

The Emotional

Do you feel me?

Our Heart is the second human discriminator, delivering the power of compassion to inform better decisions than those from intellect alone. Although Mind initially distinguishes us from the rest of the animal kingdom, it is the capacity to "have a heart" that really marks our humanity. It is quite possible to be physically and mentally powerful, yet frail in matters of the Heart. Haven't we all suffered from a knowledge-filled Know It All, that emotionally-bankrupt intellectual giant that nobody likes because he just can't relate?

The greatest thing of the world is love.
Buckminster Fuller

25 COMMONALITY
We laugh and cry
in the same language

When did we forget our common origins? I don't mean origins as monkey or divine creation (that's a debate for a different forum), but as men and women who understand what it means to be men and women in fear and hurt, and—among other things—what it means to be wrong. Attacking the details of others' lifestyles is a wonderfully subtle way to distract ourselves, and others, from our own failings. Accepting that we might not know it all, that our way of doing life might not be the only way to do life…that's the reachable and teachable way that invites cooperation and correspondingly builds real security.

We are caught in an inescapable network of mutuality,
tied in a single garment of destiny.
Whatever affects one directly affects all indirectly.
Martin Luther King, Jr.

Have you ever watched a funeral conducted by a culture different from your own, in an unfamiliar language? The trappings may seem alien, like details of color and cost, and casket-vs-cremation. The words spoken over the departed would be different from your experience, too. In one assembly, there may be loud wailing from one group, but despondent silence from another. In Iraq, for example, citizens typically behave differently when burying their loved ones than my family does in the U.S. We tend to sit quietly in our pain; some Iraqis will wail and ululate like banshees.

97

Hearts and minds...and thumb wrestling. Two humans find common ground and war loses its sting for a brief moment.

These slight differences between cultures are really not very important in the big picture.

Far more important is what is *not* different. Applied smart power seeks common ground as a starting point for peacemaking—despite the innumerable cultural layers we have developed over millennia.

For example, of those moved to tears at a foreign funeral, those whose grief exceeds their capacity to form speech, would you notice that the men wept differently from your own? Would their overwhelmed, choked expressions of emotional agony have some unusual accent compared to those in your country? No. Few sights are quite as heartbreaking as an ordinarily powerful man, broken, devastated, and reduced to wordless grief.

Would the inconsolable shrieks and sobs of women lamenting their beloved partners or children somehow lack adequate clarity to tell you what they mean?

No again. I've watched it.

Switching gears: have you ever watched a baby from a foreign culture laugh? There's no pretense; she has not yet learned the "correct" way to laugh, according to her people. Babies giggle and coo exactly as they're designed to. In some ways, we could envy them their pure humanness.

Applied smart power seeks common ground as
a starting point for peacemaking—despite the
innumerable cultural layers we have developed...

How about an adult, guffawing without guile at a particularly surprising moment of hilarity? I'm talking about that deep, sincere belly laugh that comes without warning and cannot be modulated. It's pretty much the same as yours, isn't it? Ain't nobody saying nothing…but the message comes through loud and clear.

In support of this common human experience, activist John Prendergast and actor Don Cheadle teamed up to get out the word in a constructive way on "… three of the great scourges of the world, of our time. Genocide, mass rape, and child conscription are the most deadly and diabolical manifestations of war, with the gravest human consequences imaginable." The book, *The Enough Moment* (Three Rivers Press, 2010), opens with a transcribed dialogue between the two about how they hope to motivate and mobilize their audience to act as others have done:

> Don: *They all have had some kind of Enough Moment that led them to decide to be part of something bigger for something beyond themselves.*
> John: *It is fascinating to explore what makes people care about these issues. I think some people have their Enough Moment because they genuinely are driven or touched or affected by the suffering of others, and they feel in some way, shape or form that there is some kind of responsibility…*
> Don: *Cosmic responsibility…*
> John: *The concept of being my brother's or my sister's keeper. And I think some people are driven by an imperative that is found in any faith to reach out and provide assistance to those less fortunate. Action is very clearly an essential element of any faith. I was just at a service on Sunday, and the sermon was all about the imperative to work for peace. And then, of course, there is the common security threat—you know, if we don't deal with some of these issues, then they might bounce back on us. Whether it is terrorism, disease, or environmental degradation, the issue of enlightened self-interest also can be the catalyst for involvement.*
> Don: *It will always be my hope that people will care beyond themselves, and they will want to do more. That's going to be an imperative a lot more quickly than we think it is, as some of these problems that seem so far away are going to rebound back here on us. So we are going to need to link arms with people all over the world against a greater common enemy involving environmental destruction and the ensuing lack of resources, water, and food. I mean, we cannot continue to waste as we have as a world and expect that there will be no consequence. So you need to be able to flex the*

Moments of genuine natural-ness highlight a level of humanity that we can recognize as universal.

---

muscle of altruism and humanitarianism and brotherhood and fellowship in a very necessary way. Or you know, get a bunch of guns, and hunker down and hope you got enough people with you that you can stave off the masses when they come to try to take your stuff, because it's one or the other—stand apart...united we...

John: *Hang together, or all hang separately.*

The point of all this? Moments of genuine natural-ness highlight a level of humanity that we can recognize as universal. Sex...hunger...fatigue...again, we are commonly humans. Our human instincts, drives, and expressions surface from the core of our species, in very similar ways. Look closely beneath all the layers and you will find common-ground reflections of our hearts.

Common ground is fundamental to Powerful Peace.

Consider this the next time you feel a dislike for a stranger that you can't quite put your finger on. It may just be your layers grating against his. Try instead to take a moment and imagine his pain or joy in the context of your own experience. You just might recognize a brother, disguised in an unfamiliar costume.

I opened with the concept of being Reachable and Teachable. Yes, I know the phrase reduces to the acronym R.A.T. In this context (and only this one!) I always try to make sure I'm being the best RAT I can be! Come on—be a RAT with me and inspire world-changing openness.

26 COMFORT
Peace of mind

In early 2008 I drafted the first installment of a two-year run of my monthly column, For Goodness' Sake, from the heart of war. Specifically, I wrote in a little espresso bar on a U.S. military installation in the Middle East. Thirteen months later, I returned to Northern Virginia and once again enjoyed a cup of coffee at Starbucks (which I consider my "alternate office"). Home after fifty-four weeks of urging a balanced approach in Iraq, I relaxed comfortably back in the U.S. Capital.

> **Kindness in words creates confidence.**
> **Kindness in thinking creates profoundness.**
> **Kindness in giving creates love.**
> *Tao Te Ching*

Many would ask (or have asked), "What could possess a retired SEAL to leave his loved ones again and ship off for more than a year to the hottest conflict zone on earth?" They assume it's for money. And in fact there are contractors "in theater" (assigned to war zones) who do it purely for the money, which is unfortunate; their mercenary reputation stains the rest, including those of us who believe in the mission and serve to make a difference.

However, there's another reason I go that you may not expect: Comfort.

We work not for our own comfort, but to balance out a desperate deficit of comfort for others. I'm talking the simple comfort of this coffee; or the comfort of this hometown, where you and I have no fear of death squads at the door; or the comfort of knowing emergency rooms exist and can't turn away any legitimate emergency; these are comforts we often take for granted.

I remember meeting up with an Iraqi dentist in Baghdad. He seemed too young to have been certified before the 2003 invasion and subsequent turmoil, so I assumed he had studied abroad. When I asked, he told me "Baghdad University." It turns out the school was in fact disrupted for a while after the initial burst of hostilities, but quickly got going again with a few intrepid students like my friend. Unlike students elsewhere, he had to manage the constant threat of terrorist attacks between study sessions over pizza. Context is very important. Completing one's medical training in a combat zone, or navigating a "sniper alley" just to put bread on the family table, is a context that puts ordinary American struggles to shame.

America is the taproot of liberty and democracy in the modern world. Let's remember and nurture that. I was reminded of it when I stepped off the plane from Iraq and took a family vacation to New York City, where Lady Liberty still maintains her vigil with resolute dignity in the harbor. Her courageous determination to constantly welcome victims of oppression around the globe is awe-inspiring. More of us should go and contemplate this important symbol.

Many, many non-Americans still see great promise in the American dream. Such appeal-without-effort is the foundation of soft power and forceless influence. We help ourselves if we foster it at every opportunity.

When constantly confronted by foreign (and domestic) voices broadcasting U.S. wrongdoing, it can be easy to lose sight of how much we have to offer and how much we are admired in the world. In fact, howls like "Occupy Wall Street" are only possible because of protections that are hard-wired into the national system. Yes, the United States has made missteps in its distant (and recent) history, and yes, I'm calling for accountability for all governments and all individuals as part of the solution. But let's remember how much good there is to harvest from American culture—and every culture—in building a better whole.

Many, many non-Americans still see great promise in the American dream. Such appeal-without-effort is the foundation of soft power and forceless influence.

It's for that man, and his children, and all our children,
that we need to step forward and help where we can.
Their comfort will one day translate into our own.

While the excess comfort of a so-called "couch potato" (a kinder term might be "leisure careerist") can be detrimental, some comfort is necessary for real quality of life and growth. Children need to be able to take their security for granted, if they are to develop self-confidence for a healthy adulthood. Adults need to trust they will eat tonight if they would hope to function fully around the office today.

While shopping at the Baghdad bazaar in preparation for one return home, I had a serious conversation with a local vendor. He looked me straight in the eye and said, "Why are the Americans leaving? We're not ready." In other words, he felt he and his fellow Iraqis were not adequately prepared to do it all on their own. I agreed. It would be a terrific challenge to ensure their own security (to maintain a healthy amount of comfort) and to live lives that feel right and allow no room for those self-serving, malevolent agents of misery to regain control.

It's for that man, and his children, and all our children, that we need to step forward and help where we can. Their comfort will one day translate into our own. And when the day finally dawns in a Baghdad where liberty is reality, they will be ready for a statue of their own to replace the fallen one of Saddam.

27 COMPASSION
It's the children, stupid

If babies are the purest form of human being, as argued in Commonality, their big brothers and sisters aren't far removed. Humans across the planet instinctively understand how precious our children are. In homes in every culture I've ever visited, they cherish their little ones…despite the rhetoric various populations spew to the contrary about "enemy" societies. If children require Comfort to thrive, and if healthy kids grow into healthy, productive adult citizens, isn't it plainly in each community's best interest to make this "investment" in its own future success?

Every child comes with the message that
God is not yet discouraged of man.
—*Rabindranath Tagore*

My use of the word "apolitical" to describe this preoccupation with balanced peacemaking should not be taken to mean I don't believe in politics. It means

---

...politics (and many other idols of our time) are lower, and weaker, than the unbreakable determination to make peace.

Thanksgiving in the Northern Arabian Gulf, preparing for search-and-recovery dives for drowned sailors. I missed more holidays, birthdays and anniversaries than I was ever home to attend. Americans today show soldiers great appreciation for such sacrifice. I hope we can increase compassion for the lives of others all around the world…and make our lives better in the process.

simply that politics (and many other idols of our time) are lower, and weaker, than the unbreakable determination to make peace. In fact, while many politicians loudly proclaim their devotion to national security, certain short-sighted decisions periodically lead their nations and the world farther from a stable international peace.

Nothing burns my cookies so much as watching the United States Senate, communally 100 of the most powerful people on earth, bicker childishly and toss votes back and forth across the aisle like competitors in some deranged tennis match; "49-51." "51-49." "Love."

Inasmuch as the U.S. Senate sets the course for America, and America in many ways determines the direction of the world, these national leaders affect the direction of our world. They are literally writing the course of human history. This is far too important a role to indulge in petty party squabbling. "Game. Set. Match" is utterly incompatible with global "Mind. Heart. Peace."

Far worse than childishly clannish, of course, is whorish. Whorish describes that aspect of a leader's "selling out" his constituents, and even his own conscience, for some personal gain. I suspect the most common motivator for personal gain here is simply job security; dancing with insincerity for the privilege of retaining privilege. "Elect me so I can think up why you should elect me next time." Or, "Let me rationalize some of my actions for the purpose of re-electability, without which I won't be back to serve you again the next term." This is all the more pathetic when one considers the great potential for contribution many of these talented folks would have out in society.

Note that I am not saying, "Politicians are whorish." I am saying *some* politicians are whorish. It's certainly not up to me to identify who serves and who *serves himself*

Our scripture does not say that loving my neighbor may be selectively applied based on my feelings for that person or my mood at the time.

---

among our statesmen. If you're a politician and you're reading this, you know where you stand better than we do.

Some would say I simply don't understand the intricacies of successful governance, that there's more to settling national debates than simply voting one's conscience. They would say I don't know because I haven't been in office. That's true, I haven't. Yet.

The next statement will probably burn many, many cookies, but I am convinced of its truth: Religion itself is lower, and weaker, than peacemaking. Here I'm not talking about God, Whom I consider to be above all of us and our self-inflicted wounds of dividing and diminishing. I'm talking about religion as infinite splittings of spiritual doctrine and practice among humankind. I am a believer myself, but in my belief system I'm taught that all men are brothers, and that I should love my neighbor as myself.

Our scripture does *not* say that loving my neighbor may be selectively applied based on my feelings for that person or my mood at the time. (If you have a version of the text that says such, please contact me so we can all look it up.) In fact, in my Bible there's a lot of talk about some unpleasant individuals called Pharisees. Apparently these guys loved to point out the failings of others and boast (tastefully, of course) about their own exquisite goodness. I imagine a Pharisee looking a lot like Dana Carvey's pucker-faced "Church Lady" of Saturday Night Live fame…with a beard. If you've never seen the Church Lady, you owe it to yourself to YouTube her. Carvey plays a sanctimonious little holier-than-thou congregant who blames everything she doesn't like about other people—and I do mean everything—on Satan. I hope readers from across the entire faith spectrum can appreciate how ugly and ridiculous such prideful behavior is in any religion that claims to value humility!

I know a great many Christians who act much less Christlike than the Mahatma Gandhi, who revered the teachings of Jesus Christ but never called himself a Christian. He considered Jesus a prophet of nonviolence.

Take a deep breath. Now that I've deliberately violated every social courtesy by introducing both politics *and* religion into an argument, I hope I have your attention. I also hope that, having described what Powerful Peace is *not* (neither politics nor religion), it should be easier to comprehend what it is.

It's the children, stupid.

We are an amazing race. Humans get our bloomers in a bunch on some very petty disagreements, so on the greater matters of war and terror it's important that we trace back to something we can all agree on if we desire to move forward: kids deserve better. If nothing else, kids deserve better.

Maybe someday we'll grow to a point where we can think that not only precious, vulnerable children deserve better, but that other adults (dare I say foreigners?) deserve better, too! Maybe *everyone* deserves better—better than the small, animalistic squabbling we imagine with primitive humans, when survival really did depend on reacting like animals.

Hell, maybe with enough reflection I can come to accept that even *I* deserve better…better than the miserable world I build for myself when I place my desires above others' needs. Maybe I could finally learn to act in my true best interests by realizing that my well-being is intimately connected with the well-being of others— even perfect strangers on the street. Maybe I could exercise my heart a little more and complement the workings of my mind.

A counselor friend loves to ask partners in conflict, "Do you want to be happy, or do you want to be right?" All too often, people choose right over happy. We should focus on the little things (kids, kindness, compassion), the things that are actually much larger human issues, and put our big things (ego, defensiveness, reactivity) on the lowest shelf…where they belong.

28 EMPATHY
Look through his eyes

Every baby is born with identical, basic needs: nourishment, shelter, safety, affection. From this foundation, it's easy to trace upward and understand more sophisticated human needs: a sense of dignity, self-worth, the respect of one's peers, and so on. We all share them, folks. When we understand them, and how they rise and branch out, and why they may fail to be met, we begin to understand how simple many needs are to satisfy…and how stupidly self-defeating it is to deny anyone of their needs wherever it is possible to fulfill them.

One death is a tragedy; one million is a statistic.
Joseph Stalin

Please indulge me while I briefly offer a voice to the voiceless.

I am an Afghan husband and father, a cobbler by trade. I desire only to keep my shop open, earn at least enough for basic family needs, and maintain some dignity among my peers. I know that the violent men who sometimes place roadside bombs near my neighborhood will kill me if I rat them out.

Not "kill" like in your movies, my Western friends. This is the kind of kill where men punch my face and pull me into a car, then drive me to a private place while I beg to go free and I promise them more than I have. The kind of kill where they beat my arms and cheekbones and knees and groin with sticks, then bruise my temple with the barrel of a pistol while I sob in terror. The kind of kill where they pull the trigger, and I can't just leave the theater or put another quarter in. This is the kind of kill where my young wife is suddenly and forever a widow, like many of her neighbors.

What, then, shall I do? Should I watch Mel Gibson in The Patriot *and suddenly realize that a man's gotta risk everything to do the right thing, step forward, and warn the Coalition patrol not to take this road today?*

Are you insane?

Hell, no! I'll keep my mouth shut and hope to God my family isn't harmed during this horrible plague of violence and lawlessness that's crushing my town and my dear neighbors. I've made a commitment to care for my household, and they need me. Many of you reading this have the same commitment, yet you find it easy to judge me when you don't live with the same dangers. Make no mistake: I will feel terrible that some young American's life may be snuffed out and his parents devastated…but I have my own sons to protect.…

If only this were an isolated case of individual suffering. I've actually pieced this story together from many accounts, over many years at war.

The concept of "One's Own" is a key element of happiness. The availability of adequate resources and alternatives is essential to reducing conflict. If men in an environment like today's Afghanistan have no viable means of making a living *except* supporting an insurgency, it should come as no surprise to find them joining an insurgency…for the sake of Their Own. We in the West have to break free from an Us-vs-Them perspective regarding foreign cultures in order to develop real security. Disregarding "Theirs" to ensure the well-being of "Ours" just doesn't cut it.

And I'm not talking about high-minded altruism, here, although I pray altruism can flourish and grow further out of this mindset. Here I'm talking about cold, hard, objective pragmatism. It is in "Our" best interests to deny our enemy the opportunity to drag down Our national reputation. He celebrates every clumsy mistake we make in mistreating or neglecting local citizens—it reinforces the message that he is the lesser of evils. If instead we will increase efforts to facilitate improved opportunities *at the motivating source*, we can accelerate toward an irresistible tipping point of mutual benefit. Our empathy can accelerate Their opportunity. With opportunity comes

---

We in the West have to break free from an Us-vs-Them perspective regarding foreign cultures in order to develop real security.

---

the sense of ownership for an improved lifestyle, and a corresponding willingness to defend it. The Arab Spring revolutions of 2011demonstrated this. People want to live in peace and freedom. Not fear and abuse. *All* people.

Those who should heed this most closely include any who imagine they can brutally oppress those under their care after the example of Moammar Gadhafi, Hosni Mubarak, and many other fallen dictators. In an era of radical transparency, the street is empowered like never before.

Are you not convinced? Consider my favorite anecdote on the dynamic of public security needs: While I was in northern Iraq, a common fundraising method of Mosul's AQI (al Qaeda in Iraq) consisted of weekly, house-to-house shakedowns for the equivalent of $50 each. It was a great plan: low-risk, high gain, and a steady flow of revenue. No homeowner could resist, because his life simply wasn't worth risking to protect 50 bucks—and that mob, in that environment, possessed the power to kill without consequence.

Try that same tactic in my hometown in Northern Virginia! Sure, I'd probably open my wallet and hand over the $50 to avoid having my head blown off in the moment, but before you can sashay over to hassle my neighbor John, my other friend Johnny Law will put you on the ground in an undignified and mildly painful position. Americans often can't appreciate how empowered we feel to speak out and act out confidently *only because we have already passed through a defining crucible and rejected uncontrolled lawlessness within our own borders.*

Anyone who casually declares that there will never be peace in the Iraqi or Afghan societies is simply not exercising his vision muscles hard enough. Yes, it will be exhausting. Yes, it will take a long time. (Read any account of the American Revolutionary War to glimpse unthinkable hardship and prolonged determination!) But the payoffs that accompanied transforming my town from Wild West (er…East) into the prosperous and productive society of today can be repeated, *with respect for*

Americans often can't appreciate how empowered we feel to speak out and act out confidently *only because we have already passed through a defining crucible and rejected uncontrolled lawlessness within our own borders.*

Contrast the blind use of force with great concepts that can never be killed, like the gift of cooperative democracy passed down from humanity's Athenian ancestors.

the unique culture involved, when we dare to assist troubled populations at least some way down the path we've blazed.

Don't believe the cartoon depictions of these populations. An Iraqi man is fundamentally the same as an American man—is the same as a Somali man—is the same as a Japanese man—is the same as an Uzbek man…I know! I've lived and worked among them in almost three dozen nations. I've become friends with them. Each of these men *requires* dignity and respect. We can offer dignity and respect at no cost to ourselves. He also *needs* to make a living; he *needs* to be able to put his head on his pillow at night and feel pretty good about how the day went.

If he is satisfied in such modest essentials, he'll be much more likely to contribute meaningfully at local and possibly international levels. If rule of law emboldens and supports him, he'll be much less susceptible to the intimidation and manipulation of organized brutes.

This energy, HAL (again, the fundamental "Human Aspect of Life"), is more powerful than all the bullets in the world. Vision and heart outlast force. Force will always become exhausted. "Necessary violence," which I passionately endorse, is an appropriate tool for only select, temporary conflict situations and cannot be sustained indefinitely. Force will always collapse eventually. The failed Soviet and Nazi regimes, even the global dominance aspirations of the humbled British Empire, proclaim loudly that force will not prevail.

Contrast the blind use of force with great concepts that can never be killed, like the gift of cooperative democracy passed down from humanity's Athenian ancestors. Such ideals may fade from sight while baser urges guide a region for a generation or more, but when fear and abuse inevitably reach the limits of tolerability, the higher character of our species rises from its patient slumber to risk and work for something better. When we successfully communicate this message of something better, we tap the universal human desire for security. So simple. So human. So true.

29 COMMUNITY
The Baghdad Zoo

In fair weather, Americans and Europeans love to bundle up their picnic baskets, slap on some sunscreen, and bask in the simple majesty of nature under a rich, blue sky. It's unlikely any of them will have to wonder whether their families might be torn apart, literally, by a suicide bomber racing up to detonate his car in a public park. It was big news once the same could finally be said for Iraqis in the Baghdad Zoo.

The people are all smiling; they are happy.
Adel Mousa

One of the things I love most about the privilege of living and working in war zones is that I get to see the whole picture, not just those bits our Western media squeeze in amid insistent political, financial and celebrity rehab stories. Such sound bites focus negatively on the plights of millions of humans and are often allotted fewer minutes than the entertainment segment during a half-hour news program.

Of course we need to face the bad, because that's the only way to challenge and correct it. But I want to make sure we can also see the good. Otherwise, we'll feel hopeless.

One week in Baghdad I read about the usual killings, assaults, kidnappings… then the unusual fact that the city zoo had once again become a favored family spot for thousands of Iraqi mothers, fathers, and children to spend a day of peaceful recreation. Adel Mousa, the zoo's director, expressed it best with his

With Haider after a pizza and some sober reflection on the past, present and future of his country

simple comment from this chapter's introduction: "The people are all smiling; they are happy."

At the Baghdad Zoo, these people got to feel like our people for a few hours. Nothing sells like an appealing way of life. People in every nation like to feel safe. When they do, they want more. But when safety is in very short supply, they want it even more.

Back at the Baghdad Zoo, young couples could finally stroll through shady groves holding hands and dreaming of a shared future. They could finally watch laughing, shrieking, carefree children romping on the lawn, and they could imagine one day having children together and watching them play just the same—in their own, safe neighborhoods.

Once during 2008 I talked with a Baghdadi friend, Haider, over a pizza in our U.S. base. He was less hopeful than I about the future of his tormented city, so I made him a promise I fully intend to keep: I told him that we, we all together among the freedom-loving people of the world, will do our best to overcome the destructive greed and short-sightedness of those violent or corrupt actors trying to keep Iraq unstable. That within two decades, there would be a vibrant, thriving community in a democratically-sound and culturally-relevant Baghdad which is so safe, I'll bring my children's children back and buy his family a pizza dinner downtown. He looked wistful as he said he hopes that's true.

Nothing sells like an appealing way of life. People in every nation like to feel safe.

Multi-generational families began coming back to the Baghdad Zoo to spread blankets and chat, or doze, or simply marvel at this glimpse of a Baghdad that could be again…a Baghdad that fears neither the unspeakable abuses of Saddam Hussein and his sons nor the unspeakable butchery of terrorist and criminal gangs. They could dream of a Baghdad with dignity and hope.

If we look at this zoo as a symbol of real hope and a model of release from under a cruel thumb, we are better able to estimate what we'd be willing to risk to attain it. I suspect it would be quite a lot.

Let's keep those "Baghdad Zoos" coming.

30 FAMILY
Heart is where the home is

I sincerely wish you peace, joy, and prosperity. May you have a home to live in every day of your life. It's not such a strange wish to offer these days, is it? Such difficult times. So many suffering, out of doors, at home and abroad. Take a moment and whisper a prayer for their safety and shelter…or, if needed, for yourself.

Acting is just a way of making a living; the family is life.
Denzel Washington

As I wrote this chapter in our cozy dining room, a steaming cup of liquid inspiration (coffee) close at hand and a beautiful blanket of snow draping the house, my wife was sympathizing on the phone with a lady who would soon be officially homeless. My wife, a living saint who is incapable of turning her back on any stray (yours truly included), would be "plussing up" by three cats our current stock of canines, felines and assorted rodentia. This, so three beloved pets won't go under the needle when this lady would be evicted the next day…in the days before Christmas. While the lady herself would be able to move into a shelter, animals would not be welcome at her next residence.

I pray that you will have a home to live in for the next 365 days.

Across Iraq and Afghanistan, my own alternate homes for many years, the vast majority of houses are built of stone and mortar. In most of the cities (outside of the universal, sprawling slums housing the poor), dwellings are tidy, spare reflections of the generally barren landscape seen for miles around. Yet these austere buildings hold some of the warmest, most loving families to be found anywhere on our planet.

Therefore it is not "What" the home is, in my opinion, but "Who."

Once during a year living in the north of Turkey, I visited the simple, brick-and-concrete house of my dear friend Hayri (you'll remember him from the chapter on Understanding.) His mother welcomed me as a new son, sparing no expense. And this is identical, by the way, to the generosity I've received in the homes of Americans, Russians, Omanis, Afghans, Japanese, Iraqis, and a host of other good people worldwide.

On this particular visit, I made the amateur mistake of admiring a simple, orange doily that Hayri's mother had crocheted. In less than one minute I was the proud, if somewhat perplexed, owner of that same orange doily, now neatly wrapped for transport. This was my first of many experiences with OMEH (Overwhelming Middle Eastern Hospitality). Resistance was futile; Hayri later told me I'm lucky I hadn't admired his Mom's furniture first.

The home can be a place of startling kindness, or it can contain staggering cruelty. Don't judge a nook by its cover.

The most civilized of properties sometimes host the most unimaginable evil. Witness Josef Fritzl, the Austrian father who shackled, enslaved, raped, and seven times impregnated his own daughter over an uninterrupted, twenty-four year stay in his private basement dungeon. Researching this story, I was astounded to learn that he even incinerated the corpse of one of his own infant children/grandchildren to avoid discovery.

Contrast this horror to the boundless sacrifice of countless parents in famine-stricken nations, who sometimes starve to death themselves in order to share the tiniest crumbs of food and save their children.

It ain't what—it's who.

In Powerful Peace, you've read about the importance of seeking out common ground in the quest to reduce conflict and violence. What more common ground is there than the home itself? Whether snow-blanketed like mine, or shaken by war

---

The home can be a place of startling kindness, or it can contain staggering cruelty. Don't judge a nook by its cover.

If I disdain this person's home, I have disdained him. When I honor his unique origins, I have honored him...

like those of my friends, this simple societal framework (literally and rhetorically speaking) has commonality written on it from Santa's workshop to Admiral Byrd's porta-potty on the South Pole.

In millions of homes on every continent, husbands and wives celebrate their blissful union...and quickly discover things to fight about. Children of every hue are born into homes on every terrain. Loved ones die, family cultures are renewed, and there's almost never enough money to do everything we want.

Through it all, the calendar trudges faithfully along. Seasons come and go. Life in the home, ever dynamic, remains fundamentally and appreciably unchanged, forever. I've long heard it said that "home is where the heart is," and as a man who's been everywhere else I know it to be true for me. But I also know that whoever I meet, wherever I meet him, remembers some special place, too. It might have looked, sounded and felt very different from mine. It might have been on the other side of the planet.

Home is a piece of dirt, somewhere in the world. But it is also a very real, very lasting piece of a person's life. If I disdain this person's home, I have disdained him. When I honor his unique origins, I have honored him...and I have made some little step of progress for both our lives.

31   DUTY
War heroes on war

You will hear it time and again. Those who survive war, whether behind the gun or in front of it, have a unique loathing for this uniquely terrible human process.

I hate war as only a soldier who has lived it can,
only as one who has seen its brutality, its futility, its stupidity.
Dwight D. Eisenhower

Because much of our race's history has been bloodied and ravaged by war, much has been said about war. As with Ike's opening quote, a lot of "anti-war" rhetoric has been voiced not by pacifist refuseniks, but by the greatest practitioners of the killing industry.

General Douglas MacArthur, for example, declared that "The soldier, above all other people, prays for peace, for he must suffer and bear the deepest wounds and scars of war."

General Norman Schwarzkopf said, "War is a profane thing."

Even President George Washington is quoted as having said, "My first wish is to see this plague of mankind, war, banished from the earth."

Yikes. Hating war? Praying for peace? Scars? Profane? Plague? Do some of our most accomplished and courageous warriors better deserve a title of "peace dove?" Are they afraid of a good fight?

Some of my warrior friends from Uzbekistan. We discovered upon arrival that I could teach tactics in three languages. These officers spoke English, and most soldiers spoke Russian...the village boys spoke only Uzbek, however, and Turkish sufficed for basic commands. (You can see by his stance that the man on the far left is a Russian fighter.)

I don't think so. I would argue, as General MacArthur suggests, that those who have devoted their bodies and minds to the field have developed a healthy aversion to opening this Pandora's Box because they understand how high the actual price really is. Think it's about an action star holding dual machine guns and shooting at National Guardsmen? Think again. That's a movie. It's really about little girls, families and towns being ripped apart.

It's about how to establish peace; when to use force; where to apply the lessons of history in a balanced, powerful, heartening way. Let's start with some labels: The term "peace dove" generally implies a pacifist, or peacenik, and a "war hawk" is an ardent proponent of war readiness and use. To keep this artificially simple, let's picture a hippie and a soldier...yet Eisenhower, MacArthur, Schwarzkopf and, atop the list of soldiers of renown, Washington, all condemned this thing called war.

These great leaders make it apparent that we don't need to compulsively label individuals as either Peace Doves or War Hawks at all. Some sitting at home in front of the boob tube may feel an awesome courage and willingness to pull a trigger—or rather, have someone else pull a trigger—in the assumption it means a quick end to a distant and irksome problem. Others, understandably distressed by the terrible human cost and with the best of intentions, may fight so strongly against fighting that it interferes with military readiness and paradoxically *leads to worse suffering.* These are very real extremes in the debate on force. Sadly, the debate often turns away from solution finding and toward "beating" the opposing

---

When reasonable pursuit for solutions is abandoned to political maneuvering, we fail in our duty to protect at our full capacity.

---

philosophical camp. When reasonable pursuit for solutions is abandoned to political maneuvering, we fail in our duty to protect at our full capacity.

Perhaps, as you've been reading, you've come to understand that every challenge is a distinct opportunity, to be met with courage and creativity according to its unique circumstances. We must be ready to use force whenever necessary, but exhaust all other measures first. When we hear our Commander In Chief say, "Force is the final option," we need to know this is not some political act or token statement. We need assurance that it comes from both vision and heart and reflects the best judgment of the warriors and diplomats advising. The world at large needs to understand that we will not attack while any other options are available...and that we are sincerely ready and willing to attack.

Perhaps we need a new kind of actor in the world of conflict. Perhaps we need a global network of citizens and groups and governments that pursues not a perpetual either-or debate, but a more useful balance of readiness with restraint. I founded the Peace Hawks in hopes of providing such a forum. There is a wide range of medical, humanitarian, citizen diplomacy, poverty and related organizations already serving peace worldwide. Each does important work and affects its little pocket of the world of need. When we better integrate these, and better tie in various national military, diplomatic and administrative powers, we better fulfill our duty—and fewer efforts run counter to positive intentions.

Face it. War hurts. War hurts men and women whose flesh and bone are torn by bullets. It hurts little old ladies and little old men. It hurts children profoundly to experience the horrifying shrieks of rockets, shrapnel...and to witness men and

---

...casually indulging in force reaps a corresponding harvest of ill will and cyclic violence that always returns to its source.

---

women being torn. It hurts for a child to simply go without food in a shattered land. And when a child is hurt, our common future is hurt.

Hurting all these people (or rather, permitting all these people to be hurt) by casually indulging in force reaps a corresponding harvest of ill will and cyclic violence that *always* returns to its source. "What goes around comes around," they say, and nowhere is this more evident than in the area of retaliation.

Please don't hijack my words to claim support for any particular "peace" or "security" movement. It is not an endorsement of any "side," and especially not for those least-effective "sides" at the extreme ends of any debate. This is also not an indictment of any administration, military service, government agency, political party or commercial venture.

If it is any indictment at all, it is an indictment against all of us, together; against anyone who has any say (and in a democracy each adult does) in our way ahead as a global society.

This is intended to communicate impartial, universal ideals and ideas that need to be spread. Please spread them! Ordinary citizens have power to influence the way of their nations and of the world. A condition of enduring security is not a matter for security professionals, policy makers or military leaders alone. It's a result of the conscious involvement of every person, in the way one acts and speaks...and considers consequences.

It is the duty of each of us. It begins in the Mind that is hungry to understand. It continues in the Heart that is open and compassionate. It touches the Soul, which we will touch on in the final section of this book. And it reaches the universal conclusion that if we truly want to "Let there be peace on earth," each of us must commit to "Let it begin with me."

In the end, why should some of us sweat and bleed in the training hall? Why should some be so good at putting bullets where they will do the most harm? Is this a cruel and warlike outlook on life?

To answer this, I'll defer once again to a great man whose failure would have cost not only his own life and holdings, but the very existence of a nation which now has so much to offer to the world: President Washington.

"To be prepared for War is one of the most effectual means of preserving peace."

Remember, visit PeaceHawks.org right now. Become a Peace Hawk. Make a difference.

32 SACRIFICE
How precious?

I suspect there are dear ones for whom you would willingly lay down your life. And if I thought I faced a "them or me" situation with my wife or kids, well…that would be my final thought. No hesitation. For me, then, it is easy to respond to the question posed in this article's title. "How precious?" Answer: Totally. More precious than anything I own, including my life.

Let him live…If I die…Let me die…Let him live.
From Les Miserables

Thus continued a very touching song, moving me and the entire audience during one high school musical version of "Les Miz." I didn't know the context because frankly, I was dragged to this show. I didn't want to be there and didn't care what production we were going to see…but as usual I was glad I went.

The actors referenced "barricades." From the minimalist costuming and sets, I really wasn't clear at the time about what war or revolution we were seeing. The period was immaterial. Their human experience is everything.

These words were beautifully sung by a high school girl, but I didn't know if she played a mother, lover, sister or daughter. Her role was immaterial. The humanity of her situation was universal. She was willing to sacrifice.

Anyone reading this has at least a mother and a father. Most of us have more close relatives: siblings, cousins, spouses, children. Many are precious to us...dear enough to die for.

Fast forward (or sideways), and consider other lives.

Thirty-four of the performers in that high school musical were honored because this was their final show. No more high school theater. No more high school. There were hugs, and tears, and laughter. There were obviously many people who were precious to each other. I easily understood their parents' feelings of affection and pride.

There was so much promise in that room. Thirty-four precious children, just as loved as they could be, heading out into the big world to write their own histories for their own descendants. Profound, really.

And yet....

When I fast-sideways farther from my base, out beyond these thirty-four families, I see strangers for whom I have even less affection. I may coo at the baby in a passing carriage, but forget him a minute later. This general apathy demonstrates that I could be more attentive to people, even in my own community. I have room to grow in recognizing how precious each human is.

Fast-sideways beyond my town and my commonwealth, even beyond my nation; the strangers grow more foreign still. So foreign, that if one of them dies I may hear it as sad news, rather than a tragedy. When several die, I see it more as an alarming measure—a trend.

If it were my child, it would seem like the end of the world. If we're talking about foreign strangers, on the other hand, I lose sight of that ocean of love in the heart of each and every dead child's mother, that pride bursting from the chest of each one's father during earlier, joyous times. I lose sight of the "precious" and see only a sad statistic.

As you'll read in chapter 46 on Possibility, during the evolution of the blog at PowerfulPeace.net I once made up a story about eight Iraqi children from a cute photo. With artistic license, I spelled out what I imagined to be their (future)

Promise is not exclusive to a population in North America or to any other culture. God's gifts are liberally spread across this species.

Each child we help to survive and thrive through early challenges and circumstances, therefore, is like giving our own little gift to the world...and to ourselves.

---

accomplishments: "left to right—Foreign Minister, Comedian, Restaurateur, Architect, Ambassador, President, Supermodel, Neurosurgeon."

They were the future, I said then, of Iraq. What I really meant is that they are the future of the planet. Promise is not exclusive to a population in North America or to any other culture. God's gifts are liberally spread across this species. Nurturing that promise in a child who could become a Gandhi or a Mother Teresa benefits everyone on earth...full circle, ultimately back to include those I hold most dear. Again I say, this approach to balanced peacemaking is one of the most practical, self-interested—almost selfish—activities you can undertake.

There are some things I can personally sacrifice, and others I can influence globally, such as donating to charities or giving of my time to serve in shelters and better the lives of children. If I don't exert that much effort, simply letting my mind be open to people's stories lets me be aware of them and I can share those needs with others who may be able to help in more material ways. Even if I neither act nor share, I believe it still helps the world—and my life in it—if we simply say a little prayer.

So many precious lives are chopped down young or never permitted to flourish to their potential because of circumstance. Each child we help to survive and thrive through early challenges and circumstances, therefore, is like giving our own little gift to the world...and to ourselves. It is so worth the sacrifice, and quickly becomes a way of life.

33 CRISIS
Unity through tragedy

Thank God for emergencies. Sometimes that's the only way we humans can stand to be nice to each other. I sometimes use humor in discussing general misery like the reality of terrorism and other violent tragedy. Frankly, this is because if we didn't laugh, we'd cry. A laugh can blow away the fog of dismay and bring the clarity necessary for finding solutions. It feels good.

You cannot forget your duty for a moment, because there might come a time when that weak spot in you should affect you in the midst of a great engagement, and then the whole history of the world might be changed by what you did not do or did wrong.
Woodrow Wilson

In the comedy classic, *The Russians are Coming! The Russians are Coming!* (United Artists, 1966), a Soviet submarine runs aground near a tiny U.S. New England island set in the mid-1960's. One hilarity leads to another as a small search party of Russian crewmen sneaks around the island, trying to work out a way to steal a boat, tow the sub off the sandbar, and skedaddle back to the Motherland. Before long, thanks to a few chance sightings, American little old ladies are wailing about an invasion of Russian parachutists while the sheriff struggles to restore order and the menfolk hurry to build a defense force. (Jonathan Winters is priceless as the blustering deputy who frantically shouts to "Get organized!" amid all this mayhem.)

125

When bad stuff goes down, somebody's got to go up and sort it out. Here Iraqi security forces run through an aggressive crisis response drill. Alongside my Teammates I have trained literally thousands of soldiers, in dozens of countries, in skillsets including immediate action, underwater navigation, mission planning and languages.

While I won't ruin the film by telling all the good bits or the very moving ending, I will say that this movie expertly illustrates the unifying power of crisis. Many guns do end up pointed at many apparently irreconcilable enemies, but we also see deeply adversarial relationships healed by moments of need.

It's a shame, but sometimes we need such an urgent common cause to get out of our own egos.

We read that the Titanic tragedy was another example of the finer qualities of humanity shining forth, when men of all classes unanimously assisted women and children onto a limited number of rafts with the sure knowledge that they themselves would perish. (Well, unanimously except for that one rich jerk who was trying to get Leonardo's girlfriend—but we all saw that coming!)

The massive recovery effort for September 11th involved thousands of dissimilar individuals. We never heard of anyone refusing to pull a broken survivor from the rubble because she was of the wrong complexion, faith, or sexual orientation. And when billions of global citizens and their leaders stood to condemn the monstrous evil of those attacks, there was a widespread pause in rivalries…a pause in mindless, habitual, obsolete enmities. "We are all Americans today," read the banner headline in a prominent French newspaper.

We never heard of anyone refusing to pull a broken survivor from the rubble because she was of the wrong complexion, faith, or sexual orientation.

> Many hands make light work.
> Many minds make light of heavy challenges.
> Many hearts make light in a dark world.

Wouldn't we like to feel that again, but without the senseless loss of innocent life? Wouldn't it be nice to rise above our perpetual squabbling over crusts and focus instead on making truckloads of fresh pies? Many hands make light work. Many minds make light of heavy challenges. Many hearts make light in a dark world.

I have criticized some in Congress for its divisive diversions in mismanaging this country through petty pursuit of personal gain. Granted, that esteemed body is an easy target, but isn't this justifiably so? After all, don't those coveted seats exist not for privileged rulers over a nation of subjects, but for the first servants to all others in this great experiment of democracy?

The partisan Senate vote is a pitiful sight. Such vast power spent opposing the Other, often to protect political territory. Couldn't that tremendous energy be harnessed and aligned to press forward, instead of sideways? There is a finite amount of strength and a finite amount of time available to each lawmaker. Every ounce of strength and every minute spent in actively opposing another party on principal is an ounce and a minute that can never be recovered to find best solutions to problems of the economy, national security, health care, and any number of other needs of the population. The waste is outrageous when you begin to consider it. Can there be any doubt that we would have accomplished more on such crucial issues if not distracted by political maneuvering?

I'll continue to challenge our leaders when they don't serve us, and if it ever comes to pass that I become a member myself...I'll self-subordinate further and dig even deeper for the courage to be even more critical, pressing for something that works for the benefit of all citizens.

I believe it is possible to work together without waiting for crisis. In fact, I've watched it happen in dozens of countries around the world.

We have the capacity to look beneath the surface of another, whether from our point of view he has too many earrings or not enough, and uncover that person's unique potential...potential which, again, could contribute to our own best interests. In practice, however, it's much more common to judge a book by its cover and react to the differences. This is where we misuse our sense of personal power and lose out on the Other's potential to contribute.

I am the first victim of my contempting another. I discard a person who might otherwise be able to help me at some point. Is such contempt based on his appearance, or some affiliation?

Am I not then perpetuating unproductive, partisan thinking?

I propose that we apply smart power at the individual level. Let's open our minds, look for the value in those unlike ourselves, and discover how alike we are. This is "Smart power to the people!" We can learn to work together without a reliance on crisis for motivation. As with any preventive maintenance, proactive cooperation invisibly and automatically averts some crisis. A positive cycle—a virtuous, not vicious—cycle is born.

If you take nothing else away from this chapter I urge you once again: please watch *The Russians are Coming! The Russians are Coming!* Seriously. You could use a good laugh.

34 DUALITY
And

"Balanced budget." "Balanced breakfast." …Balanced peacemaking. What is it about this simple word? Balance is important to economics, medicine, athletics, academics, governance, and every other aspect of the human experience. So why is it so hard to practice?

**Integrity without knowledge is weak and useless,
and knowledge without integrity is dangerous and dreadful.**
Samuel Johnson

Pop quiz:

According to doctors, which is an essential component of healthy weight loss: diet, or exercise? Great, you got it right: diet *and* exercise.

According to advisors, which is an important part of financial health: saving more, or spending less? Right: saving more *and* spending less.

Why should it be any different with interpersonal or international relations? Balance is necessary, and the operative balancing concept is *And*.

In the world today we find incidents of horrifying *and* inexplicable violence… *and* I don't have to be sitting in Iraq to tell you about it. In 2009 a hateful old white man carried a gun into the Holocaust museum in Washington, DC and gunned down a young, black guard in the prime of life. This victim, eulogized as a kind and gentle giant, had sworn to defend the lives of strangers at the risk of his own. He

---

If he had reached the gathering and detonated, soldiers and children alike would have been torn to pieces.

---

was murdered for being born a certain color, or for protecting a Jewish memorial, or for both.

The young man's fellow officers responded appropriately. They returned fire, critically wounding the murderer and eliminating a threat to everyone else present.

Regular readers of our ASP blog at PowerfulPeace.net are familiar with the following scenario: U.S. soldiers in a war zone, handing out candy to local children, are approached by a nervous young man in a bulging coat. The soldiers escalate through the "force protection" procedures demanded by military authorities (Shout, Show your weapon, Shove…and only then Shoot); yet he begins running toward the group.

A soldier puts a bullet through the young man's head. He falls, dead on the spot. As security forces investigate the scene, they discover that he was in fact concealing a shrapnel-filled explosive vest. If he had reached the gathering and detonated, soldiers and children alike would have been torn to pieces.

From such accounts, the occasional need for the "hardest" power of full kinetic action is apparent. Without necessary violence, much greater suffering of innocents would have followed. In this case, "*And*" included the use of deadly force.

The soft power of example and attraction is as necessary to balanced relationships as the capacity for force. Indeed, it is more powerful, because modeling compels and convinces more genuinely than coercion.

One of the best media examples of duality is clearly labeled as such. In the Vietnam war movie *Full Metal Jacket* (Warner Bros., 1987), Private Joker is challenged by a Marine colonel for wearing a peace symbol button and having "Born To Kill" scrawled on his helmet.

Joker: "I think I was trying to suggest something about the duality of man, sir."
Colonel: "The what?"

"The duality of man. The Jungian thing, Sir."

"Whose side are you on, son?"

This exchange continues for a few lines, at the end of which the colonel confidently declares, "It's a hardball world, son. We've gotta keep our heads until this peace craze blows over."

And is a very important tool in our kit for connecting both likes and dislikes. *And* speaks to our similarities as much as to our contrasts. At the very least, *And* demonstrates a link between two ideas or people and a chance for change. It shows what we are…and what we may become.

It says such things as, "I hate *and* revile you."

It can also say, "I used to think thus and so…*and* now I think differently."

Such a tiny word. Such profound meaning.

35 EXCLUSION
Are you with us or against us?

On the occasion of being mildly assaulted by a fellow American who thought I was "just" a local Arab in the Middle East.... Our inherited, status quo thinking pattern about the value of others can create perpetual, self-inflicted misery.

We have kept on because we strive for harmony and community, a community not only of the living but also one that honors our forebears. This link to the past gives us a sense of continuity, a sense that we have created, and create, societies that are meant to be for the greater good and try to overcome anything that subverts our purpose. Our wars end; we seek to heal.

Desmond Tutu

Powerful Peace is *apolitical*. I want that to be understood before initiating the following sensitive discussion.

The title of this chapter is not a criticism against President George W. Bush for using similar, strong words immediately following 9/11. Neither is it an endorsement of his comment, which should simply be considered in the context of that terrible and historic time.

This is a story about a man who bumped—no, slammed—into me at the airport in Kuwait.

In a bizarre turn of events, I was moving with a group of Americans through a crowded terminal and found myself momentarily blocked by a second man, who was being momentarily impeded by a third. It was a simple people-jam, and would resolve within seconds. In profile, the bearded man just in front of me looked surprisingly like my Egyptian friend Kamy (remember the chapter, Context 3?), but at that moment I was thinking the odds of this being Kamy were statistically impossible.

My musing was abruptly interrupted by what can only be described as a low-impact, hockey-style body check by the American behind me, as he literally bounced my 220-pound frame out of the way so he could hurry to catch up to the group. I kept my cool (probably not as well as I like to think) and followed close behind. Once I caught up I got in his face and said, "We're all going to the same place. There's no reason to slam into anyone!"

He looked thoroughly surprised at the American English coming from my own shaggy beard, and began to apologize. Unfortunately, the apology was even more unacceptable than the initial body slam.

"I'm really sorry, dude. I didn't realize you were with us!"

I was stunned by this response.

With us?

What the hell difference would that make?

With us??

I knew that by "us" he meant the American group (I wasn't "just some local Arab"). I could have taken the apology for what it was worth—despite the stink of blatant (and probably unconscious) bigotry. But this brief encounter is an invaluable teaching point for Powerful Peace, so it swirled in my mind until I could return to the keyboard and write down this lesson: There is no "us."

Of course, there are blacks and whites, men and women, Jews and Muslims and Christians...that's not what I'm saying. All these distinctions are part of the natural, healthy, perfect mosaic of what it means to be complementary pieces of the human race. The point is that there is no "us" in the context of his apology. Us-and-

---

Us-and-Them thinking deserves to go on the discard pile of useless history alongside its evil cousins, slavery and genocide.

Them thinking deserves to go on the discard pile of useless history alongside its evil cousins, slavery and genocide.

You see, what the American did in that crowd was to define, by deed, his own counterproductive understanding of We and They. Without a word, he demonstrated that he finds it acceptable to smash into Them to get where he wants to go, but not into Us, the group of which I happen to be a member.

"They" don't deserve respect, and "We" do. It seems to be that simple.

While this occurrence is offensive enough at first glance, the deeper and much more profound effect ripples outward and begs to be examined.

When a person behaves like that in a place like that, the locals very reasonably find it intolerable. While they may not confront the offender as I did, they inevitably file it away in memory. When on a different occasion another visitor behaves in a similar manner, resentment grows. At some point a prejudice is formed against my *entire* group. A prime example comes with the term, "Ugly American," which must be based on a long series of unacceptable events. Such a widespread reputation didn't cross the globe because of one or two isolated incidents.

Some such events are harsh and widespread. Others are more subtle and confined, like this example from my own editor: Rob was in Moscow in 1996 with his wife and newly adopted, Russian-born daughter. They happened upon other American couples who were also seeking to adopt children in need of loving homes. The group invited Rob and his family to join them at Pizza Hut (a by-product of *glasnost* and *perestroika*) in order to "get away from this awful Russian food." Rob was appalled. His family had experienced three weeks of ORH ("Overwhelming Russian Hospitality") and sacrifices including wholesome, farm-fresh meats, fruits and vegetables, which Rob's wife Virginia called "to die for." More appalling was that the group's inconsiderate invitation was made in front of Rob's Russian translator, Olga, a fluent English speaker. Sensing Olga's hurt feelings, Rob turned to her and said, "Ugly Americans! We have some, you know," then whisked Olga and his family off to more respectful surroundings.

The upshot of this dynamic is that, when I again pass through such a "culturally contaminated" area, my own experience will be unavoidably colored by the attitudes of these prejudiced locals. I may get poor service; I may be harassed; I may even be assaulted by some of the more hot-headed youths. No matter how effective my usual efforts to "get along" in every environment, they may be overcome by the thoughtless, offensive choices of others.

We each need to get better at considering the potential consequences of our choices.

This threat extends also toward the safety and peace of mind of my spouse, my child, and other companions....

Most stupidly of all, even that bigot's future experience in that place will be impacted by his past behavior.

We each need to get better at considering the potential consequences of our choices. We are an amazing race, the humans. Our species has the capacity for infinite, creative genius...and yet even the dumbest dog won't defecate where he sleeps.

By the way, in case you were still wondering: yes, it was Kamy in front of me in line. I met up with him and had a great talk a half hour later.

36   INCLUSION
Colores

My friend Eduardo Sanchez and I used to enjoy climbing up onto the roof of the "Victory" Palace in Baghdad to relax in the evening over good cigars. During one such talk, I mentioned the article that would become this chapter. He suggested that since it was a multi-cultural story, I title it multi-culturally. Thus: Colores (Colors).

> **We understand that the long journey of democracy is one that is best made by people of all nationalities, ethnicities, religions; that together, we are a stronger mosaic of democracy than we would be if we were homogenous.**
> *Condoleezza Rice*

It's probably tough to participate in organized racism throughout most of America today. The combined face of our society has become so beautifully diverse, one might feel there's nowhere left to safely gather and plot!

In all seriousness, though: if you are a dedicated race hater, please give me three minutes and consider this chapter. It's my strong wish that you'll stop fearing the

---

A moment of reflection costs nothing, but may reward you with lasting returns.

I was the integrator for combined work between this Arab aircrew and their ground element, which was also trained by my platoon. We make a pretty diverse bunch, much like our 9/11 SEAL platoon...complete with unity of purpose.

integrated cooperation of humans and try to imagine that other points of view may, at least theoretically, offer some small value in the quality of your life.

A moment of reflection costs nothing, but may reward you with lasting returns. Put another way: you don't have to like me, but if I'm not an imminent threat, your own life would be so much more pleasant by simply ignoring me. Active opposition is so...active!

Now to the backstory of this weighty introduction: I dashed home from Iraq for a few days one June to honor the scholastic achievements of my children. Sitting in one elementary school assembly, my attention wandered (as usual) and I began to study the fantastic ethnic diversity in that sea of bright young faces.

In Iraq I see faces like those in that auditorium. I've also seen faces like these in Pakistan, Somalia, Thailand, Russia, El Salvador and Hong Kong. My American hometown (and yours in Chicago, Houston or Sacramento) is the face of the world!

There was every combination of colors and features I could imagine. I realized, with sudden deep and humbled gratitude, that these kids will never know the racial illiteracy I experienced growing up in a small, very ethnically white, Upstate New York village near Canada.

...these kids will never know the racial illiteracy I experienced growing up in a small, very ethnically white, Upstate New York village...

These kids, whatever their future difficulties with friends, lovers and bosses (hopefully not all the same person!) will never be handicapped by such total ignorance of other cultures. They'll never be easily provoked into unnecessary conflict based on racial misunderstanding.

In other words, their lives will be healthier and of a much higher quality because of this hour in this auditorium, and thousands of hours like it. Best of all, they'll never know the ignorance they've never known!

Around the world we look, speak and celebrate differently from one another. Yet how different are the foundations of these simple human experiences?

Each group has a cultural range of beauty. Some, at one end of the spectrum, are called attractive. Others, at the opposite end, are…well, like me!

Our speech differs, but we all use speech to ask, buy, scold, teach, and convince. Regardless of taste, my need to eat is identical to that of my most distant international neighbor. As for the amazing variety of human celebrations, well, who doesn't love a good party?

At the level of the heart, we are the same worldwide. At the level of the American population, we uniquely exemplify the entire spectrum of human types and possibilities. Yes, the blending comes with its own challenges and yes, in my opinion there's real value in honoring and celebrating one's unique cultural heritage. I, for one, am very proud to have French, Norwegian and Celtic roots. Yet this in no way diminishes my capacity to admire and explore *your* unique roots in Peru, Japan or Belgium. The key to a strong society lies in learning to honor mine while appreciating yours. Like twigs in a bundle, each of us is stronger when aligned and connected than when arranged in opposition.

INTO ACTION PLAN III

- Read Prendergast, *The Enough Moment*
- Log on and join up at <u>PeaceHawks.org</u>. Become a voice for balanced peacemaking.
- Watch *The Russians are Coming, the Russians are Coming!*
- If you haven't already, read through the Holy Bible *with a study guide*...and do the same with the Holy Qur'an. Many people are surprised at how much they have wrongly assumed is—or isn't—contained in each.

SECTION IV
SOUL

The Moral

We've got spirit, yes we do!

The Soul is our third and highest human discriminator. While Mind and Heart are adequate to distinguish man from beast, the moral compass of a well-developed conscience marks both our humanity and our capacity to be "humane." Intellect alone is neutral. It has inspired great cruelty. Passion alone lacks discernment. It has led to wildly imprudent choices. When we grow to accept the guidance of conscience it complements our smarts *and* our hearts. At this point we are able to—and desire to—make our greatest contribution.

**We cannot solve our problems with the same
thinking we used when we created them.**
Albert Einstein

37 TOLERANCE
In defense of faith

Where did it come from, the rampant, wild-eyed tsunami of Islamophobia? In the U.S. we heard the refrain against Muslims: "They are waging a stealth jihad against America!" Across parts of Europe, nationalism reached a fever pitch.

Even though the world is divided by many particularisms,
we are united as a human community.
Kofi Annan

Islamophobia 2010 was clearly a reaction to the proposed "Ground Zero Mosque." I won't weigh in on that explosive debate in this brief chapter. The point is that the mosque war caused some unacceptable and ironic casualties against deeply-held American values called freedom of religion and respect for diversity.

Before you leap out of your breakfast nook and shout that I'm labeling that Islamic center a topic of "religious freedom," let me reiterate: this is not about that facility. It's about the fact that we jeopardized religious freedom *because of* a debate about religion.

My two-part response to The Question that The Muslims are Waging a Stealth Jihad against America:

Answer Part A) **Yes**...there is a stealth jihad underway.

Think about it: any group sophisticated enough to carry out the complex attack of 9/11 is smart enough to come at the problem (us) on multiple fronts. They told us who they are: al Qaeda. And AQ said it speaks for all of Islam.

Remember that Hitler said he spoke for all good Germans. Remember, too, that through the skillful manipulation of grievances and fears, he whipped up a fever pitch against another cultural-religious group, that he accomplished this through impassioned nationalism…and that the German language root for "nationalism" led to the term "Nazi."

Answer Part B) **No**…it's not *"the Muslims"* who are after *"us,"* any more than cop killer Eric Rudolph and his Christian supporters could be interpreted as proof that *"the Christians"* are out to murder abortion doctors.

Now think about this. If you identify yourself as Christian, do you also automatically consider yourself a member of "Christian Identity," the movement that believes all non-Whites go to hell? Do you identify with Pastor Fred Phelps, the patently un-Christlike founder of the "Westboro Baptist Church" and its "God Hates Fags" movement? They have waved signs celebrating war deaths at military funerals and laughed at family members as they suffer in grief…this includes families of my fallen SEAL Teammates. I've communicated directly with members of the Phelps clan in hopes of comprehending the incomprehensible hatred of these self-described Christ followers. I've included a portion of that dialogue, with permission, in the next chapter. Read it and be reminded of Hitler's hate speech from the 1930s and 40s. You'll get a glimpse of a part of history that, if forgotten, we will be doomed to repeat.

There are unsettling similarities between today's warnings to WATCH OUT for *Them-There Muslims* and der Fuhrer's earlier hysteria-laced speeches warning about the menace of *Them-There Jews*.

Remember your neighbors as human beings. Before 9/11 (committed by a tiny handful of radical, *self-described* Muslims), millions of Muslim Americans lived within a society that had overcome widespread suspicion about a global Jewish conspiracy (thanks, WWII!), a disgraceful era of state-sponsored segregation

---

There is a difference between "Muslim" and "al Qaeda." All AQ members call themselves Muslims, but very few Muslims want to be AQ.

against blacks, and the surprising election of a Catholic as one of our most beloved presidents of all time. Muslims serve in the U.S. military and politics alongside Hindus, Buddhists, and atheists.

There is a difference between "Muslim" and "al Qaeda." All AQ members call themselves Muslims, but very few Muslims want to be AQ.

I have read the entire Bible...twice. I've read the Torah, and I have read an English interpretation of the Qur'an. It's good to understand what different people believe. (One uncomfortable factoid is this: most Christians haven't read the Bible from cover to cover.) All these stories are similar. Each faith appeals to the soul through the language and culture of its adherents.

Some challenge the claim that Islam is a religion of peace. They say it's not like Christianity because it's full of violence. Hang on a second while I look through the scriptures of my own religion...ah, here it is! *Joshua 6:21*, in summing up the delightful story of God's explicitly-choreographed, ruthless and gory conquest of Jericho: "They devoted the city to the LORD and *destroyed with the sword every living thing* in it—men and women, *young and old*...." [Italics mine.] There's more about genocide and mandated violence in there. Much more. And for those contemporary Christians who argue that the Old Testament doesn't "count" any more, since it was replaced by Jesus' ministry, I ask: is it part of our Holy Bible, or not? If it no longer applies, then what motivates today's condemnation of Old Testament "abominations?" If it does still provide mandatory instruction, why aren't those rules universally applied within the church?

An impartial reading of Leviticus, a book shared by both Jewish and Christian traditions, reveals fundamental laws not very unlike those of Islamic "*sharia*." Yet "creeping sharia" alone raises howls of protest in some segments of society. We ought to fish or cut bait on the Old Testament question. Nothing creates well-deserved bemusement and incredulity from outsiders like apparent hypocrisy and double standards within the church.

This appeal is not intended to raise Islam above Christianity, or vice-versa. I'm merely asking that we pause in our daily drama to consider where each of our fellow humans is really coming from. I do believe in God, and I do believe God made us all. I'm also pretty sure that each of us is flawed and sees only a small part of the whole picture. A friend once described religion as a "spiritual metaphor," a tool that helps us define the indefinite. I like that idea very much. The problem arises when this tool, laid down through forms of revelation and tradition and innovation, is confused to be "all" that can be said or thought about God and God's intentions.

Not one of us is big enough, brothers and sisters, to declare that we individually hold all of God's truth. I suspect God finds our presumption either very amusing, or very irksome.

During one great cigar-enabled conversation with my SEAL friend Dave Brayden, he put the whole thing into perspective with a clarity (and brevity) that I lack: "It was easier when we were kids. We watched the cowboy movies and the news, and they were the same—we always knew who was wearing the Black Hat. Someone has to wear the Black Hat."

Let's search our hearts humbly before slapping the Black Hat onto a billion of the world's people.

38 HOLY WAR
I'm sorry for what we've done to ourselves

Following a particularly productive engagement with a local Coalition leader at Camp Victory in Baghdad one day, I set out for a tranquil, cool-sunny afternoon stroll back to my office at the al-Faw (also known as "Victory") Palace. Walking alongside the shimmering palace lake, I felt drawn to stop by a mosque I'd noticed earlier en route. According to custom—and military law of protocol—I did not enter the facility (I have been accompanied into others by Muslim friends), but I did poke my nose in from the outside. My buoyant mood was transformed into an anchor.

There is not a single offense which does not, directly or indirectly, affect many others besides the actual offender. Hence, whether an individual is good or bad is not merely of his own concern but really the concern of the whole community, nay, of the whole world.
Mohandas Gandhi

I have always wandered, and I am always saddened to discover abandoned houses of worship for any religion in my wanderings. These are centers of community and

---

I am always saddened to discover abandoned houses of worship...

These are centers of community and hope that just aren't doing their important work anymore.

---

hope that just aren't doing their important work anymore. Each represents a place in which crime, poverty, or in this case war, have diminished a local population's ability to satisfy its needs to assemble and develop their faith in that Something greater than us all.

Each of these places has seen its former occupants of self-sacrifice and generosity replaced by dust and bird droppings. Most, of course, are not physically scarred by the wounds of violence as this one was. I can't know which "side" is responsible for slamming high caliber rounds into a wall of this building and blowing out some of its handcrafted windows. Probably both sides. In Afghanistan, entire neighborhoods have been leveled by heavy weapons; 95% of that ordnance was fired by Afghans of one group or another. Despite the physical devastation of these communities, the people still live there…it's all they've had, and it's all they have.

I'm reminded that our shared loss is not limited to this formerly-beautiful building, or to this type of damage. Isolated American soldiers displaying very poor judgment have shot bullets through the Qur'an, or otherwise mistreated it, for provocative effect on Muslim detainees. Some have made deliberately abusive comments about Islam's most-revered prophet, Mohammed. (FYI for the uninformed, Muslims also revere as prophets Moses/Musa, David/Dawud and Jesus/Isa.)

Nor is the loss limited to Islam at the hands of non-Muslims. Self-described Muslims have pointedly massacred Christian and Jewish men, women, and children. They've done the same to the "other" kind of Muslim (e.g., Sunni on Shi'a or vice-versa). In a seemingly insane hypocrisy to male and female purity, some have even brutally raped women of their own "kind" of Islam in the name of Godly discipline. In Northern Ireland, under the same cross, Protestants and Catholics killed each other for many years in a faith-divided political struggle.

And, of course, the loss is not limited to faith on faith. Some individuals take great pleasure in attacking beliefs not to their liking, such as Andres Serrano's photo of a crucifix in a glass of urine entitled *Piss Christ*. (No, I won't show that particular piece of "art" in this book. You'll have to Google it yourself.) Self-described Christians have murdered abortion doctors and innocent bystanders at public gatherings. As mentioned in the previous chapter, the "Westboro Baptist Church" is one particularly fringe Christian group whose members verbally abuse mourners at military funerals. Also as mentioned, I've corresponded directly with them in hopes of discovering/defusing some of their destructive motivation. I was told, "7 billion people hate our words," and, "You can huff and puff until God takes the last breath from you, and stops your beating heart which he holds in his hands, with the most high-minded rhetoric you can drum up—and hate us with all your being—and bad mouth us all over the world—and that changes nothing. We. Aren't. Going. To. Have. This. Nation's. Blood. On. Our. Hands. We, like Noah and all the brethren in the Scriptures, are going to obey God, and warn our fellow man that the proud institutionalized sins of this nation are taking this nation to ruin."

Frankly, such a self-righteous sense of entitlement to rampant cruelty is more frightening to me than any number of well-ordered military divisions. At least with a military, there's some hope for a rational solution.

In what author Reza Aslan calls "cosmic war," there is no hope for a rational solution. In *Beyond Fundamentalism; Confronting Religious Extremism in the Age of Globalization* (Random House, 2009) he wrote:

> "The events of 9/11 by no means inaugurated the debate over religion and violence in the modern world, but they did render the issue unavoidable. It is easy to blame religion for acts of violence carried out in religion's name, easier still to comb through scripture for bits of savagery and assume a simple causality between the text and the deed. But no religion is inherently violent or peaceful; *people* are violent or peaceful....
> "A cosmic war partitions the world into black and white, good and evil, us and them. In such a war, there is no middle ground; everyone must choose a side. Soldier and civilian, combatant and noncombatant, aggressor and bystander—all the traditional divisions that serve as markers in a real war break down in cosmic wars. It is a

---

...such a self-righteous sense of entitlement to rampant cruelty is more frightening to me than any number of well-ordered military divisions.

---

simple equation: if you are not *us*, you must be *them*. If you are *them*, you are the enemy and must be destroyed.

"Such uncompromising bifurcation not only dehumanizes the enemy, it demonizes the enemy, so that the battle is waged not against opposing nations or their soldiers or even their citizens but against Satan and his evil minions. After all, if we are on the side of good, they must be on the side of evil. And so the ultimate goal of a cosmic war is not to defeat an earthly force but to vanquish evil itself, which ensures that a cosmic war remains an absolute, eternal, unending, and ultimately unwinnable conflict."

Personal attacks on others' personal beliefs hurt the offended…and ultimately, they hurt the offender, too. Whether at the local level of damning differing beliefs as cultish, or actively participating in hatred at the level of cosmic war, this is just one more form of sowing seeds of discord. They bloom as thorns of destruction for everyone involved. In a way, this is sort of like punching a window in anger. The destructive power may feel good at first…but you're likely to end up with some very nasty—and unnecessary—cuts.

39 CAMARADERIE
Surrounded by armed Turks!

Armed Turkish soldiers encircled me, the solitary American. They moved closer, speaking their strange language. I was acutely aware that I had no weapon other than my own two hands. Abruptly, we all paused at the first sounds of a running machine gun battle closer to the center of Baghdad. That fight wasn't far from my "hooch," a half mile from where I stood....

Deep down, we know that what matters in this life is more than winning for ourselves. What really matters is helping others win, too.
Fred "Mister" Rogers

The above introductory incident is all true, but I'm pleased to report that I am neither dead nor captured. In fact, I'm very comfortably tucked in with a cup of gourmet coffee and a keyboard.

And now, The Rest of the Story:

In dozens of countries around the world I've been blessed to live among international forces. I have always explored their cultures with the curiosity of a child. In the early 1990's, my assignment to Turkey lasted a year. (This was coincident with the collapse of the Soviet Union, but I won't take credit for that one.)

I would drink *chai* in the tea gardens with best friend Hayri, that same long-suffering Turk whose mother had foisted the orange doily upon me during my first visit to their home. We would talk for hours about his father the *imam* (religious

151

On the left of this photo is "Zhenya," then-commander of Russia's Spetsnaz (Special Forces). I'm the grinning fool in the middle, and on the right is "Sasha," the Spetsnaz intelligence chief. You are welcome to interpret that any way you like.

leader), the quality of carpets in Hayri's rug shop and, all too often, about how horribly I had most recently offended nearby little old ladies with my inadvertent Turkish mispronunciations. (During the first months Hayri frequently had to hustle me off to various tea gardens to escape the scorching glares of victims of those linguistic drive-bys. Turkish has some very simple words that sound like sounds I quickly learned not to make.)

Years later, after losing contact, I learned that Hayri had also made his way into the military—also as a commando. He led a squad in the southeast against Kurdish fighters of the PKK, designated as a terrorist organization by Turkey and other nations.

(I've got friends on both sides of this Kurdish question, so if you write to me to tell me how wrong the Turks are and how right the Kurds are, be forewarned: I will be receptive and understanding. One of my cutest snapshots of kids from around the world, in fact, is of little Kurdish waifs in their enclave outside a Turkish town.)

It's funny how a gentle, small town preacher's son would end up in my industry. It's funny how people from across the entire human spectrum can come to be involved in violence against strangers. Our natural instincts to protect "our own" against dangerous "Others" expand to include institutional Us-vs-Them functions at the national level with militias and armies. We can be gradually taught to hate the "Red Menace" and become willing to "Kill a Commie for Mommy." The other side learns to loathe the "capitalist pig." (I imagine us eventually splitting down to

I once hosted Zhenya Khayev, the head of Spetsnaz (Russia's version of our SOCOM, or Special Operations Command), in my backyard for beer and hot dogs.

the lowest common denominator and having seven billion independent states with names like "Larry" and "Elizabeth" replacing today's Peru and Ireland.)

I once hosted Zhenya Khayev, the head of Spetsnaz (Russia's version of our SOCOM, or Special Operations Command), in my backyard for beer and hot dogs. We spoke in Russian about how pleasant it was to not be enemies for the time being. We also discussed how, should our international relationship degrade to war again, and we find ourselves face-to-face on some distant ridgeline...only the quicker trigger will walk away. Duty is like that.

Rewind to those armed Turks surrounding me in Baghdad. These were actually liaison officers from the Turkish Army, friends of mine, and not adversaries. They were hosting a "Hail and Farewell" party for a change of staff. They had invited me and a variety of international colleagues; I enjoyed speaking Russian with the Ukrainian and the Georgian, Turkish with the Azerbaijani and our hosts, some Arabic with the Jordanian, and English with the rest. Sure, I was unarmed, because at the time I was only working as an advisor in the palace headquarters of General Petraeus. (This was in two *different* offices of the palace, you understand. Completely different floors, actually.)

Also true is that, with these Turkish friends surrounding me, we paused the party and listened to a running machine gun battle a half mile away near my hooch...it was *outside* our base wall, but just barely. While this celebration of ours represented the harmony possible among a dozen very different partner nations, men were savagely killing each just other within earshot. While war raged on those ancient streets, "micro-globalization" in one tiny trailer in Baghdad, Iraq—or in one

While war raged on those ancient streets, "micro-globalization" in one tiny trailer in Baghdad... showed a flicker of hope for the future of this race.

suburban backyard patio in Hawaii grilling hot dogs—showed a flicker of hope for the future of this race. It is one possible direction for the future of humanity...but it will not spontaneously occur; we will have to choose to act. We will have to choose camaraderie, or we won't have it.

40 APPRECIATION
Credit

"Credit" may seem an odd subtitle for a peacemaking theme. After all, isn't this book about the need for mental and emotional balance in applying smart power? Especially in troubled years, when the economy is on everyone's mind and the misuse of credit has been a major contributor to the problem, this might seem a touchy subject.

The 30th day of May, 1868, is designated for the purpose
of strewing with flowers, or otherwise decorating the
graves of comrades who died in defense of their country.
Earliest United States directive on the observation of Memorial Day

This chapter is not about money. We may hear expressions like, "To his credit, he is one heck of a softball player," or, "The family dog was credited with alerting residents to the deadly kitchen fire." Credit can be a good thing.

So I was sitting at the Veterans' Administration (VA) clinic, having finally found enough time to get my post-retirement medical exams done. On the wall was a small poster testifying to the importance of the organization's mission. A simple photo showed the torso of a very old man standing in a suit, with a special focus on his ancient, gnarled hands…and a U.S. Congressional Medal of Honor around his neck. The caption said, "Serving those who served."

As a veteran, any honor given to our earlier veterans (who sacrificed more than I'll ever know) gets me all choked up. During one World War II commemoration

---

Credit and commemoration...should not be limited only to those who have fallen, or only to those in the military, or only to one special day a year.

---

hosted at my SEAL Team when I was on active duty, some WWII "frogman" vets came to visit. They were stooped, wobbly and quiet...yet I knew they were some of the toughest men this—or any—country has ever seen. While today we tote around millions of dollars' worth of high-tech gear and reap the benefits of near-unlimited training budgets, they quite literally faced hails of gunfire wearing only shorts and a knife.

These original combat swimmers, called "UDT" for Underwater Demolition Teams, were established to destroy submerged enemy obstacles positioned on key enemy beaches. In dive shorts and masks these naked warriors would surface swim toward an occupied shoreline, then dive on breath-hold to tie on explosives and blow up underwater obstacles—a skill set we continue to practice today. When the waters were truly frigid, they merely applied an insulating layer of grease to their bare skin and soldiered on.

One of these ancient heroes approached me and said how much he admires our generation for all that today's SEALs can do. I laughed. I told him we see it exactly opposite; they paid a monumental price to lay the foundation for this legacy of sacrifice and service; we just try to live up to the example they set. We are the "Sons of UDT."

America's Memorial Day is celebrated to remember military members, like those early SEALs, who have paid the ultimate price in giving their lives. Credit and commemoration, however, should not be limited only to those who have fallen, or only to those in the military, or only to one special day a year.

Credit should certainly be extended to those who courageously waited (and courageously wait today) for their beloved spouses and parents to return from war. A stable home is a priceless gift to a deployed service member, and invaluable to society itself...for today, and especially for tomorrow.

A stable home is a priceless gift to a deployed service member, and invaluable to society itself...

Credit is also due to those who serve in daily life. The cleaning man who smiles cheerfully while going about his work deserves our active, spoken appreciation. Librarians, too. And what about the unpaid or underpaid public servants, those local officials we elect but barely compensate to take on the headache of governing the generally uninvolved and perpetually ungrateful mass of the rest of us?

While we're at it, let's look for chances to give credit to people whenever they do something right. A well-placed "atta boy" costs the giver nothing, but provides a boost for the receiver and can even "go viral" through his subsequent contacts to benefit many you'll never know about.

Most importantly, are you giving enough credit in your own home? Give credit everywhere it is due—and watch your own human credit score climb.

41 MINDFULNESS
Words as hands

Sticks and stones may break my bones, but words will never hurt me. Bull. Words hurt just as easily as sticks and stones, and the wounds can persist and spread for generations.

> **They got together and swore a pact to the devil. They said,**
> **'We will serve you if you will get us free from the prince.'**
> **True story. And so the devil said, 'OK, it's a deal.' …But**
> **ever since they have been cursed by one thing after another.**
> *Pat Robertson*

Pastor Robertson made few friends in the Caribbean with his comment that 100,000 Haitian men, women and children died by earthquake and disease, and millions more were ruined…*explicitly because the country sold its soul to the devil in the 18th Century.* Of course, it's likely his response to this would be that he doesn't care whether he makes friends while doing the Lord's work, because God tells him

---

It does strike me as very odd that God would create billions of people, then give all truth and wisdom to a few hundred, few thousand, or few hundred thousand.

---

directly what to do, and "feel-good" is not a motivating factor. I hear that destructive dismissal from some of the holiest rollers in every religion.

It does strike me as very odd that God would create billions of people, then give all truth and wisdom to a few hundred, few thousand, or few hundred thousand. Does God *want* us to fight and mutilate one another? As Star Trek's token Vulcan, Mr. Spock (who probably never believed in any deity anyway) would say, this is "illogical."

I just wish Pastor Robertson would reference his sources. It's a pretty specific accusation, with apparently non-specific sourcing. Did he witness this discussion with Satan first-hand? Or did some old guy who'd never been to Haiti tell him what he himself had once been told by some other old guy who'd never been there? My guess is it's the latter. As for being "liked," I agree that following one's mission shouldn't be driven by its popularity. Some of my own friends have asked to be removed from announcements about the blog at PowerfulPeace.net, so I know as well as anyone that you can't please all the people all the time. But if the good preacher wants to serve in this world as directed by the Master described in the scripture we both follow, he should probably try out a little more open-heartedness to offset an apparent predisposition for casual condemnation. Nobody can do much good who sounds like a Pharisee/Church Lady.

You may remember the fury around the opening quote while public revulsion was still pulsating. I'm not digging it up for cheap drama, but to establish a premise. The "words can never hurt me" adage seems as bogus to me today as it did when I was a child, and for one inescapable reason: words can most definitely hurt. Granted, they may not break my bones like those pesky sticks and stones…but on the other hand, sticks don't cut like a knife.

Pastor Robertson's comment could be described as a "slap in the face" to merciful, compassionate humans everywhere. I suspect that to Haitians, his words feel more like a kick in the nuts.

It's interesting to note how many of our expressions relate words to physical effects. I can "lift you up" with the right words, or I can "smack you down." All without actually lifting a finger! My wife reminds me that words can "comfort" a child, just as if we held him. With a few well-chosen words I can close your eyes for slumber, or I can shake you awake.

Words play a big part in applying smart power. What we say to or about one another creates a perception as real as the physical monuments we raise with our hands. Words fashion an impression, and impressions flow into action.

I've been physically struck many times. None of those blows, however, had the same effect as the (mercifully few) times when words have "floored" me like "a punch in the gut."

When I hear such thoughtless obscenities as, "We should just bomb the Middle East into a glass parking lot," I sometimes ask if the speaker would be willing to travel back there with me so he can pick out the first little girl to die under the first bomb. This rhetorical question often turns out to be a conversation killer.

In my various professional and extracurricular roles I've been physically struck many times. None of those blows, however, had the same effect as the (mercifully few) times when words have "floored" me like "a punch in the gut." I've never been knocked out by getting slugged, but I have occasionally been "staggered" at hearing horrible news.

The right words can make the strongest man cry like a baby. My wife also points out that words can have a "crushing" effect or "break" a heart. Many professionals will recall having been "stabbed in the back" by an ill-intentioned colleague.

I have to admit I was somewhat skeptical about Pastor Robertson's declaration that our all-merciful God mutilated thousands of babies because of a deal made by their government two centuries ago. I'd like to ask: would he be so eager to rationalize the infernos, tornados, earthquakes and other "acts of God" that periodically wrack our own country in the United States?

Since I understand he likes to teach from one book above all others—and since I happen to keep that same book right on my nightstand—I decided to crack it open and see what it says about caring for suffering people. I came upon the 12th verse of Colossians 3: "…clothe yourselves with compassion, kindness, humility, gentleness and patience."

Those words ring a little truer, I think, than a glib pronouncement that an entire nation is under murderous judgment. Pastor Robertson's comment sounded more like Pastor Phelps than Jesus Christ. I can imagine the 12th verse of Colossians inspiring the tireless work of many hands, carrying hope instead of damnation to the hurting Haitian people. But I can only imagine our introductory quote (that all Haitians had it coming because of a discussion from generations before their births) leading to a paralyzing apathy about inconceivable human agony. I speculate that the

Westboro Baptist Church people would cheerfully line up behind this message…but is that really the cheering section he wants to have?

I'd like to share one final group of words, extracted *verbatim* from an online forum discussing this unloving comment that a nation of men, women and children deserved to be destroyed for an ancient, probably mythological conversation by their government:

"I'm 13 and I use 2 go 2 church until my parents saw this. They panicked and didnt want me to end up like that…."

Is the loss of this lamb a success in the eyes of the shepherd who caused it?

42

HUMANITY
Fighting fighting

Once it's possible to perceive one's similar characteristics—one's shared humanity—with another, the base is laid for common ground…and reduced grounds for conflict.

> I felt everyone else was a lot smarter. I worried about my physical
> and mental inadequacies…. Just a few days before some of these
> were rising young executives. Some were farmers, some were
> salesman, drifters, blue-collar workers. A few days before they
> had been many things. But at the induction center [we] were all
> alike…. I discovered people are alike in many, many more ways
> than they are different. I discovered the other fellow is pretty
> much like me. He likes good food, he misses his family and
> friends, he wants to get ahead, he has problems, he wants to relax.
> *Quoted by David J. Schwartz*

Does any of this not make sense? The above passage from *The Magic of Thinking Big* (Fireside, 1959) demonstrates how simple it can be to begin understanding humans from divergent backgrounds; how simple it is to discover common ground with strangers and their societies.

In contrast, and as introduced in chapter 5, *Fixing Intel; A Blueprint for Making Intelligence Relevant in Afghanistan* (CNAS, 2010) was published about five decades later by Major General Mike Flynn while he was the senior military intelligence

Women in some parts of the world have absolutely no opportunity for a fair say in society…or even to be heard in public. In this picture from post-Baathist Iraq, that paradigm has shifted. Just ahead, in Chapter 44, you'll learn even more about the necessity of valuing both gender halves of society.

officer in Afghanistan. I've quoted this paper many times, because like some other commanders he is demonstrating the principles of Powerful Peace in real time. We cannot succeed through relying solely on "kinetic" operations, with which many military leaders are most comfortable.

This evening I read a portion of the opening quote to my wife and explained (as she's endured countless times before) that this universal human experience is a cornerstone of ASP thinking as a means of reducing conflict and improving security. "Three billion men," I droned on, "want basically the very same things from life. Each wants to have a little fun, hang out with buddies, make a living…."

She added, "He wants to be accepted."

He wants to be accepted.

See, that's why I try to never write anything without consulting her first. Her practical insight puts me on topic like a laser pointer. But what else would you expect from the world's most gifted (and compassionate) special education professional?

We all want to be accepted. The desire for acceptance is a driving factor in every choice to affiliate, whether among the Boy Scouts or the Crips. If you're an Afghan man who sees the Taliban as the only game in town, where else would you find your affiliation (not to mention your necessary paycheck)?

Critics of applied smart power often label the attempt to understand motivations as being "touchy-feely." Some misconstrue that it means we can hold hands and

---

We all want to be accepted. The desire for acceptance is a driving factor in every choice to affiliate, whether among the Boy Scouts or the Crips.

"...it does provide elements of even greater strategic importance—a map for leveraging popular support and marginalizing the insurgency itself."

---

sing Kumbaya with enemies. It is anything but touchy-feely. Never forget that ASP is based on leveraging the best balance of coercion and persuasion, or hard and soft power, for each situation. If a suicide bomber is approaching our ECP (entry control point, or "base gate"), my only appropriate response is the hard power of a bullet between his eyes. He won't change his mind at this late date...so I'll have to reconfigure his mind for him.

The difference between uselessly touchy-feely and an urgently needed soft power of understanding is being recognized by commanders downrange and back in the Pentagon. Mike Flynn and his *Fixing Intel* co-authors illustrate vividly our available resources to understand the population:

> "This vast and underappreciated body of information, almost all of which is unclassified, admittedly offers few clues about where to find insurgents, but it does provide elements of even greater strategic importance—a map for leveraging popular support and marginalizing the insurgency itself."

In other words, if the (social, economic, security) health of a population is increased, the disease of insurgency (which relies on those imbalanced factors, or unhealthy tissues) is reduced. This is basic preventive medicine.

During one assessment I conducted around Afghanistan, I asked a young bookseller in Kandahar how the Taliban, one of the world's best examples of a worst way to govern human beings, could possibly hold their own against the unprecedented military might of the Coalition. He replied immediately, "Because men don't have jobs." This wise young man went on to tell me that in some damaged communities, the Taliban have been able to forcibly recruit one man from *every* household—under threat of murder.

We can reduce the support base for our enemy by better relating to his society. When locals understand that we understand them, it eliminates some of his "home court advantage." This is especially true when he is already violating local customs and mores. If all else fails, an improved understanding of the enemy's cultural situation can help us better go where he desires to go…and more effectively stop him with hard power actions. We can learn to see through his eyes, as I have done in my work to emulate terrorists. This helps us kill him better, when that course is absolutely necessary—right between the eyes.

And conflict is certainly not limited to war. Again, in the boardroom, bedroom, or battlefield, misunderstanding leads to unnecessary fighting, destruction and retaliation. *Understanding*, then, is the medicine for the malady of conflict. It is readily at hand—understanding even grows naturally in the wild—but it is all too infrequently administered.

43 ACTION
Entering Indonesia

It's all well and good to talk about "applying" smart power, but what would it look like in practice? This chapter lays out an appeal I published immediately following the devastating Indonesian earthquake of September, 2009.

In the final analysis, our most basic common link is that we all inhabit this small planet. We all breathe the same air. We all cherish our children's future. And we are all mortal.
John F. Kennedy

At PowerfulPeace.net on October 2, 2009 I posed an argument that the United States should hasten into an aggressive and well-publicized (bear with me—this is a benevolent self-promotion) humanitarian response. I addressed it to the president, departmental secretaries, Congressional representatives and senators, and patriotic Americans everywhere. I said that "the gauntlet has been thrown down by Circumstance. Our honor, obligation, and privilege is to respond in force."

Samoa, American Samoa, and Indonesia had been devastated by earthquake and tsunami effects. Hundreds lay dead, thousands staggered injured and homeless. I wrote, barely twenty-four hours past the second set of lethal tremors, that "we must seize the gauntlet with fierce determination."

America has promised the world change. America has promised the world a more balanced, more effective, more human engagement on every front, including

> ## This terrible human tragedy was an excellent opportunity to walk our talk. *It was our greatest opportunity to help ourselves.*

in even the harshest realities of terrorism and insurgency. This terrible human tragedy was an excellent opportunity to walk our talk. *It was our greatest opportunity to help ourselves.*

Again I affirm, for what seems the millionth time: violent conflict is an expression of grievance. Somebody's mad about something. It may be a perceived wrong, a perceived inequity, or a perceived neglect. The perception may be completely inaccurate, or it may be 100% correct. Getting to the root of fighting means getting to the root of grievance, the only level at which true change can occur. Until that elephant in the room called 'grievance' has been acknowledged—most especially by the perceived wrongdoer—we can only expect to escalate in strike and counter-strike.

Those who most strongly oppose the United States and other Western nations see only a partial picture. Like great salesmen, they actively highlight our occasional abuse of power where we're not needed, and our neglect of power where we are, as proof that we are bad.

Within counterterrorism circles, it is a common observation that Indonesia has the world's largest national Muslim population. It is also noted that the hostile, anti-U.S. segment of that huge Muslim population is small, per capita. (In fact, four out of five Indonesians polled have reported having an improved opinion of the United States because of earlier tsunami relief efforts.) It makes sense to focus our energy on this massive, influential and receptive-to-influence group in need. Is there a better population, or a better time, to demonstrate our commitment to make the world better? Is there a better way to hamstring Muslim extremist claims that America wishes to wage war on Islam?

I hypothesized: "Somewhere, right now as you read this—not tomorrow; not when we get our act together and mobilize in a few days—a little girl is trapped, terrified, and suffering under the rubble of the building where disaster claimed her. She's alive…right now. If she is rescued because of our immediate action, the ripples of goodwill and gratitude from her family will flow to our very shores, and splash on anti-Western sentiments in distant lands. If instead of just one, we assist in recovering thousands of endangered men, women and children, the celebration of her story will be magnified thousands of times over.

"If on the other hand we do nothing, or reserve our full capacity in favor of a token gesture…well, her grieving family's tale may be incorporated into our enemies' deep reservoir of anecdotal rhetoric that America is a heartless giant."

This argument urged that we "strike the real enemies: ignorance and misunderstanding." We should un-cloud the vision of a skeptical world regarding what we know to be America's genuine golden character.

The argument appropriately addressed Secretary of State Clinton, who had used the expression "smart power" ten times during her confirmation hearing speech. We ought to turn our vast resources against such urgent challenges, beginning the process of healing that begins with broken limbs and extends to international relations and evolved counterterrorism. The ripple effects of our visibly acting in the best interests of global need flow through generations.

I addressed Secretary of Defense Gates as well, saying that we don't have to have the entire army ready to go, in order to start. "A few are ready now—let's send them. As recovery efforts grow and more responders are prepared, we can send them. We can establish an adaptive, modular command and control (C2) process to layer in progressive coordination over time."

Is there risk in such a scenario? I guarantee it. Indonesia has organic terrorist groups. (I use the term "terrorist" carefully, because all too many media outlets do not. We aren't talking about outgunned resistance forces using IEDs to attack military units. These are *actual* terrorists, including those in al Qaeda, who actively seek the death and mutilation of harmless families. They use the IED against peaceful markets and houses of worship.

Yes, the risk is significant to our response teams from the U.S. and other nations. In my Red Team work, acting as a terrorist cell to reinforce security programs, I have personally exploited the high emotional value of executing spectacular attacks against unprepared populations. Even if the only victims are a handful of children or medical staff, the subsequent withdrawal of a damaged organization is rewarding and provides excellent propaganda material. Witness the claims of AQ to "defeating" the United States when soldiers are killed. Witness the dramatic shift and retreat from Iraq of Spanish forces following the Madrid train bombings, and the jubilation among the supporters of those murderers. In these cases the IED is a weapon of *strategic*, not only tactical influence.

"Are we ready to be the America of this world's dreams? That little girl's waiting."

Such groups, more focused on perverted ideologies than on the desperate human need of their countrymen, are likely to consider this an opportunity of another sort—to make a name for their movements of corrupted thinking.

Yes, risk is inevitable, but the likelihood of being attacked is low. By virtue of strength in numbers, the broader our rescue mission, the "safer" each responder is individually. Indonesia at that moment represented a macro version of the "bad neighborhood" many cops prefer to avoid…the better cops enter anyway. They answer the call to serve and protect, and in so doing they hold back the spread of chaos and suffering.

I ended that (unheeded) appeal for applying smart power with a challenge: "Are we ready to be the America of this world's dreams? That little girl's waiting."

44

PARADOX
War is good

From leaping into action for humanitarian reasons we turn to leaping into action with the necessary intent to destroy. Sometimes the worst we can imagine turns out to be a blessing. A family suffers financial ruin, then finds its true riches come from one another. A tyrant brutalizes his subjects, then (when all other options are exhausted) courageous nations initiate what Washington called that "plague of mankind"—war. The paradox of conflict includes also the need to integrate women into the male-dominated culture of war, and the martial artist's understanding that sensitivity helps us fight better and end war sooner...with less destruction.

> **If the only tool you have is a hammer, you
> tend to see every problem as a nail.**
> *Abraham Maslow*

I hope the subtitle hooked you.

It is a true statement. Read through to the end and you'll see the point.

I'm a retired SEAL, so you can believe this: I'm not squeamish about the readiness and willingness to cause harm. It's a simple fact of life that there are some in this world who target innocents and won't choose to stop. They can only be stopped. Someone must be prepared to stop them.

While accepting this cold reality, we need to respect another: governments with the means to stop those who harm innocents have to be conscious of the potential

Yamaji dojo, c. 2009: I'm third from right in standing row; also standing, with goatee, is my good friend and very dangerous teacher, Corey Capone; behind the yellow belt is Corey's even more dangerous teacher and the master of our school, George Parulski. Corey's daughter Devon Hayden stands at far left; my sons Gabe and Jack kneel/stand at far right.

consequences of their use of force. Put another way, the worthy surgeon knows his tremendous power to heal with a knife must be managed with tremendous care, because misuse of his gift may cause injury or even death.

No doubt about it; there's plenty of room for debate on the question of how much hard power is appropriate. There can be no debate, however, that it's absurd for innocent bystanders to be hurt as a consequence of our protecting innocent bystanders.

As Maslow said, "If the only tool you have is a hammer, you tend to see every problem as a nail." I see this one-tool dynamic at work in the behavior of some of my fellow soldiers and in the imaginations of some soldiers' supporters. To be effective, however, we need as many diverse tools as can possibly be assembled. Most of them are not designed to kill. Many are intended for building up households, neighborhoods or regions.

What I'm trying to say should be pretty obvious: whatever idiocy we adults may choose, the children whose flesh and spirit are torn by our petty struggles deserve to have us fight much, much harder…toward better solutions. Restraint is possible, and careless fighting spawns fighting.

…the worthy surgeon knows his tremendous power to heal with a knife must be managed with tremendous care…

> To be effective...we need as many diverse
> tools as can possibly be assembled. Most
> of them are not designed to kill.

There is another tremendous paradox inherent in conflict. War and violence instinctively stimulate rigid and closed resistance by those threatened...but solutions are most easily discovered through open sensitivity to the root causes of a conflict. War is traditionally the domain of men, and men traditionally reject sensitivity as an acceptable behavior or identification. In discussions on the topic of women and war at the U.S. Institute of Peace (USIP), the New America Foundation (NAF) and other venues, we have reached two conclusions:

Firstly, "women's" issues in war are unique to females, yet simultaneously universal. Consider the epic tragedy of mass sexual violence waged strategically against a population. The immediate victims are (*usually*) women and girls...yet the terrorizing effects are often targeted against the men in their lives. Husbands, fathers and brothers of potential or actual rape victims are emotionally damaged along with the emotionally and physically traumatized female victims. These men are often responsible heads of households. They often hide their families or flee with them instead of stepping forward and participating in armed resistance.

I'm humbled to be acquainted with Abigail Disney, filmmaker of the documentaries *Pray the Devil Back to Hell* and *Women, War and Peace*. Her work is at once heartbreaking and inspiring. Women—and men—Abby shows us come through as incredibly powerful, courageous and resilient human beings instead of helpless victims.

The other inescapable conclusion on women and war is that males have too long dominated in this arena. Perhaps a better way to say this is that if women had enjoyed a more equal voice in governing the affairs and disputes of state throughout history, there would have *been* less war.

Three of my other female heroes co-edited the USIP book, *Women and War* (Endowment of the United States Institute of Peace, 2011). Kathleen Kuehnast, (Director of USIP's Gender and Peacebuilding Center of Innovation); Chantal de Jonge Oudraat (Director of USIP's Jennings Randolph Fellowship program); and Helga Hernes (Senior Advisor on women, peace and security issues at Oslo Peace

Research Institute) are highly accomplished individually; but in this partnership their results are inspiring. Their active and able cohort on gender issues and war is Gayle Tzemach Lemmon. Gayle is the author of *The Dressmaker of Khair Khana* (Harper, 2011), the true account of an enterprising Afghan woman, her family and their town under the Taliban.

Abigail, Kathleen, Chantal, Helga and Gayle personify the insight and ability necessary to build powerful peace. While on the subject of gender and conflict, of course, as mentioned in chapter 19, I strongly recommend *Half the Sky; Turning Oppression into Opportunity for Women Worldwide* (Alfred A. Knopf, 2009).

The value of sensitivity in conflict won't surprise those with experience in traditional martial arts. Since my earliest military days I've practiced various Japanese and Korean fighting styles, and consider my "home" art to be *jujutsu*— the hand-to-hand style of the Samurai warriors and parent of today's karate, judo and aikido. To put it mildly, an insensitive *jujutsu-ka*, (jujutsu practitioner) is a losing jujutsu-ka. Success depends on maintaining a quiet mind and relaxed body, effectively turning oneself into a living, breathing sensor. The more sensitive a martial artist, the earlier he can perceive an intended threat, respond appropriately, and survive.

I like the description provided by Jonathan Maberry in *Ultimate Jujutsu; Principles and Practice* (Strider Nolan Publishing, 2002):

"The word Jujutsu may be translated freely as 'the gentle art,' but the word 'gentle' is often misunderstood, a result of poor translation from centuries ago. A more accurate translation would be, 'the art of gaining victory by yielding or pliancy.' Gentleness refers to the art's approach to self-defense, as well as to the spirit of the warrior. A gentle spirit is one that does not seek to fight, and in modern Jujutsu this is the very core of honor: to fight only in defense, and never through desire, or anger, or hatred.

"The ultimate goal of Jujutsu is *not* to kill, or even maim. Rather, it is to control a situation so that it never becomes violent. This requires common sense, a balanced ego, courage and a keen knowledge of psychological cause and effect. Sometimes violence is unavoidable, and in those circumstances the Jujutsu-ka has a variety of available defenses depending on the level of threat, from simple non-destructive control techniques to far more severe responses."

Sounds a bit like Powerful Peace, doesn't it? Readiness to fight, combined with determined restraint. The pursuit of victory without force.

Sensitivity allows an individual to literally "go with the flow." Conflict is, at its core, resistance. In jujutsu we happily go with the flow and make full use of an opponent's resistance energy. If he pushes, I get out of the way and pull. If he pulls away, I push him faster and farther than he intended. This push-pull, pull-push harnesses available energy and magnifies the "resources" (energy and motion) available to accomplish my goal of no longer being in a fight. And flow itself is very important. Stopping and starting not only steal valuable time in a critical situation, but discard the kinetic power of momentum.

One final diversion to reinforce this concept of paradox; with this one, I hope to throw your comfortable mental state and assumptions right to the mat. (That's jujutsu humor.) My own personal "guru of stress-free productivity" and supporter of Powerful Peace is David Allen, author of *Making It All Work: Winning at the Game of Work and Business of Life* (Viking Adult, 2008). In his original, wildly-successful personal productivity process and book, *Getting Things Done* (commonly known as "GTD," Penguin Books, 2001), he points directly at the same concepts as acquired through his own martial arts experience. Here they are applied to management of the self:

"In karate there is an image that's used to define the position of perfect readiness: 'mind like water.' Imagine throwing a pebble into a still pond. How does the water respond? The answer is, totally appropriately to the force and mass of the input; then it returns to calm. It doesn't overreact or underreact....

"Anything that causes you to overreact or underreact can control you, and often does. Responding inappropriately to your e-mail, your staff, your projects, your unread magazines, your thoughts about what you need to do, your children, or your boss will lead to less effective results than you'd like. Most people give either more or less attention

---

Conflict is, at its core, resistance. In jujutsu
we happily go with the flow and make full
use of an opponent's resistance energy.

War *is* good...but for one thing, and one thing only: establishing a secure peace.

to things than they deserve, simply because they don't operate with a 'mind like water.'"

David's simple explanation of the ineffectiveness of reactiveness and imbalance in daily tasks is immediately translatable to the realms of interpersonal and international conflict:

> "Reflect for a moment on what it actually might be like if your personal management situation were totally under control, at all levels and at all times. What if you could dedicate fully 100 percent of your attention to whatever was at hand, at your own choosing, with no distraction...?
>
> "It's a condition of working, doing, and being in which the mind is clear and constructive things are happening. It's a state that is accessible by everyone, and one that is increasingly needed to deal effectively with the complexity of life in the twenty-first century."

To me the linkages are obvious between an awareness of gross abuses against women, the martial artist's appreciation for balance, the management of the self and the practical conflict reduction of Powerful Peace. We humans are far more connected than not. Grasping this connectedness allows us to understand both our real ability to act for positive change and a real sense of responsibility to do so. Being "connected" is so significant to daily life and conflict that another important book has been written under that very title. We'll come to that closer to the end.

Returning to our original paradox: War *is* good...but for one thing, and one thing only: establishing a secure peace. As stated in our dojo, "avoid rather than check...for all life is precious and no one has the authority to take it away." An intolerable wrong like Hitler's conquest must be confronted, but no healthy person desires a perpetual state of war. A powerful peace does not come about by accident but by deep sacrifice, willingness to seek middle ground, and a reasonable sense of urgency. It results from pouring our souls into the efforts of restraint and considered response...no matter how much we want to kill back.

45

OPPORTUNITY
Civil affairs

My friend Munira El-Bearny is a Kenyan immigrant to the United States and runs a center for newly-arrived refugees through a Department of State program. Munira has a big heart, but she doesn't take it easy on these families fleeing religious, political or wartime hazards. She likes to say, "We give a hand up, not a handout." An old American expression reminds us that what is given cheaply is valued cheaply. Beneficiaries need to have some sense of ownership—some "skin in the game"—if they are to appreciate and make the best of second chances.

There's a whole lot of humanity out there
that the average American will never be able to see.
Rob DuBois

This opening quote is the first line of an email I once sent to a colleague in another part of Iraq, who was involved in a Civil Affairs (CA) function. Yes, I know. It's lame to quote myself. Unfortunately, nobody else had said just what I want to get across here!

CA is the military mission that seeks to care for basic human needs within a host population. In this case, the civil affairs project involved a classroom in a small village. The team was teaching Iraqi women, aged 25 to 55, to read.

I acquired a photo of this class. I won't show it to you; I deliberately left it out. Although the photo perfectly illustrates one aspect of hope for this troubled people, and although this particular image is well worth its thousand words… it's classified. And it's classified not to protect national secrets, but the students themselves. If identified, any one of these women might have been deliberately punished in town by beating, rape, or even murder—for striving to claim a future for her children—by some brutal, self-imposed local guardian of "decency." How's that for mixed messages?

75% of the ladies in this class are widows. Remember, their average age is only 40! Three out of four forty-year-olds have already lost their husbands. They are individuals of fierce strength and courage, burning with a vision that their children deserve better. They risk as much as any mother could.

Since this photo is so meaningful, and since we can't print it, I will try to "show you" the picture with words. I will try to help you see the brightness, the dreams, the colors, and one small child shimmering like a jewel in the foreground. I will try to help you see the future plainly visible in the present.

There's a rich theme of greens throughout. Green is the traditional color of Islam. The cement floor is a mottled green; the visible right and front walls are in two-toned shades of green. Sunlight floods through open windows and reflects from an old, green chalkboard propped up with old, green chairs. There is even a green, two-liter soft drink bottle used to carry drinking water by a lady who cannot afford anything else. With the exception of their faces, the women wear black from head-to-toe. They sit raptly attentive. One stands at the board, chalk in hand, carefully practicing the Arabic letters that can unlock the world for her children.

Staring innocently and shyly at the camera is one tiny girl. This little girl (we'll call her "Wahida"), as small children tend to do, is leaning back toward her source of certainty—the loving care of her mother, who peers intently at the chalkboard. Except for Wahida's tragic familiarity with the savage violence and torn bodies of war, she is no different from any American two-year-old. She even has a little pacifier hanging from a little string.

In contrast to the greens of the room and the black shrouds enveloping the mothers, Wahida is an oasis of brightness. Her big brown eyes and short, reddish hair frame a cherubic face. Her orange shorts and blouse dance with pretty flowers and lace; she even has little matching sandals. Wahida is a fragile symbol of this

---

They are individuals of fierce strength and courage, burning with a vision that their children deserve better.

Wahida is a fragile symbol of this region's awesome potential. In another two decades she might be finishing a degree in Economics at Baghdad University...

region's awesome potential. In another two decades she might be finishing a degree in Economics at Baghdad University, eager to burst forth to take on the world and eternally grateful for the many sacrifices of her tireless mother. Baghdad might then be once again a thriving, bustling center of hope for this part of the world, much like the Tokyo of 1965. These things just might be. It's not impossible.

I'd like to crassly conclude by quoting again from my email that opened this chapter: "You know where the hope of the world lies? In that beautiful little girl facing the camera. We just have to give her hope, first."

46 POSSIBILITY
Tomorrow in our hands

I hope you'll indulge a fanciful flight of optimism. I have a fierce belief that we can and will overcome the limits of today, as generations before us have sometimes done— limits in our ability to trust and risk; limits in our ability to imagine; self-inflicted limits in general. It's a little-known fact that the U.S. Navy SEAL training program was established on the premise that a man can go ten times further in mind and body than he believes possible. That's why we don't swim several hundred yards at a time; we swim several miles. It's why we don't do twenty pushups for punishment; we do two hundred.

**I have a dream that my four little children will one day
live in a nation where they will not be judged by the
color of their skin, but by the content of their character.**
Martin Luther King, Jr.

I don't think limit-smashing should be limited (pun intended) to SEAL training. SEALs are just men, and men are just humans. Humans have the capacity to shatter their limits across the board. We forget that visionaries like the Wright brothers were considered crackpots for years while they challenged widely-accepted limits that mankind would never fly. Without the irrepressible determination of a few crackpots, the world would be much different than it is today.

Iraqi kids and my fanciful predictions for their future lives: (left to right) Minister of Foreign Affairs, Famous Comedian, (tallest) Restaurant Owner, (tiniest) Architect, (looking aside) Ambassador, (center) President of Iraq, World-Famous Model, Neurosurgeon

I, for one, will not permit my mind (my thoughts and beliefs) to be reduced. I will believe larger, and larger, and larger to help the material world become as it should be; it should be better than it is right now.

This is so urgent, because I have a difficult confession to make. I'm dying.

…Oops. Sorry. Let me rephrase that: I mean, I *will* die. We all will. In a way, we're all dying, all the time. Why don't we let that tick-tick-tick inspire us to act fully, to "live out loud," with the time we have left?

As Mel Brooks said, "If Shaw and Einstein couldn't beat death, what chance have I got? Practically none."

We all know we're going to kick the bucket, whether in a few minutes or a few decades. If when I kick that bucket the world isn't somehow better off because of my little flicker of life, what a tragic waste it will have been.

As you read in this chapter's opening quote, a great American once said, "I have a dream." Well, I and many others share that dream. You probably do, too.

It's high time we followed his example. He knew it was risky to say what he needed to say. He could have stayed home and watched TV that day, instead of going out to say what we needed to hear. He could have stayed home, but he didn't. He could have stayed home another day, but he didn't…and he was shot to death for trying to bring all people together.

Humans have the capacity to shatter their limits across the board. We forget that visionaries like the Wright brothers were considered crackpots for years...

> I will not subordinate my dreams and our future to fear and doubt. Dreams are the only part of tomorrow that we own today!

This single person's dream energized decades of transformation. How much greater, then, if you and I and everyone else picked up and carried that willingness to dream—and *act*—according to our most life-producing imagination? Robert Fritz wisely said, "If you limit yourself to what seems possible or reasonable, you disconnect yourself from what you truly want, and all that is left is a compromise."

I will not subordinate my dreams and our future to fear and doubt. Dreams are the only part of tomorrow that we own today! The only limits to what *might* be are those we choose. Since goals pull us toward some version of what we seek, why accept any goal smaller than greatness?

47 PROACTIVITY
Co-create your world

In one lifetime, at different moments, I've been hurt physically, mentally, emotionally and spiritually. A lot of that hurting, much to my dismay, came in the form of reactions—reactions from others or from the natural environment—to choices I had made. This is the proverbial burnt hand caused by touching a hot stove. Sometimes I had been aware of those potential consequences, and on some occasions I was blissfully ignorant beforehand...most of the time I knew better. It may be the same with you.

**If one is lucky, a solitary fantasy can
totally transform one million realities.**
Maya Angelou

Imagine that I'm standing at the train station for a day trip. Imagine I'm carrying an overcoat, umbrella, satchel and coffee. I'm feeling rushed because I missed the first train, so when the next arrives and the doors slide open I am very eager to board. Another man is also trying to hurry on, beside me.

Stop.

We're going to diverge for two possible alternative scenarios and explore the two ways I may choose to literally create my immediate future.

Scenario A: I shoulder past the man trying to board in front of me, successfully winning the right of way to get on first. With a suitably disdainful

183

glance at my defeated opponent, I ascend the steps and assume my rightful position in a choice seat.

I fail to notice when the $50 ticket slips from my overloaded hand and flutters to the platform....

Scenario B: I begin to board, but hold back in order to make way for this other fellow who's obviously also in a big hurry. In the moment he realizes I'm weighed down with stuff, he pauses and insists I go ahead. I gratefully proceed up the steps and settle into a good seat.

I fail to notice when the $50 ticket slips from my overloaded hand and flutters to the platform....

Stop.

Now let's rejoin our story in progress and examine the possible outcomes of these two choices.

In Scenario A, my fellow traveler happened to notice the ticket fall from my hand. With a malevolent grin, he smoothly kicks my ticket off the platform to be lost on the tracks below. As he passes my seat, his delirious smile makes me seriously wonder about his state of mind.

In Scenario B, my fellow traveler happened to notice the ticket fall from my hand. My new friend snatches up the ticket I dropped and heads straight for me. "Hey, buddy, you dropped this. Better be more careful," he says with a genuine smile. I'm spared a serious hassle. I might have been charged again, to buy a new ticket on the train; I might not have had the funds available and been removed at the next stop; I might have spilled coffee all over myself in a frantic search of my belongings (heed the voice of experience). Any of this was prevented because I took a moment to be considerate of another.

Nicholas Christakis and James Fowler are co-authors of *Connected; How Your Friends' Friends' Friends Affect Everything you Feel, Think, and Do* (Little, Brown and Company, 2009). What impressed me most about *Connected* is their assertion that:

> "The great project of the twenty-first century—understanding how the whole of humanity comes to be greater than the sum of its parts—is just beginning. Like an awakening child, the human superorganism is

---

Any of this was prevented because I took a moment to be considerate of another.

Did I not *create* the environmental conditions
I experienced over those next ten seconds?

becoming self-aware, and this will surely help us to achieve our goals. But the greatest gift of this awareness will be the sheer joy of self-discovery and the realization that to truly know ourselves, we must first understand how and why we are all connected."

Although my train platform scenario is a fictitious exercise of imagination, most of us can easily trace out the logic of the outcomes. Many of us can easily recall a real-life example of offensive behavior biting its owner. Maybe we don't think about this enough, but our choices clearly lead to both short- and long-term consequences, for good or bad. Did I not *create* the environmental conditions I experienced over those next ten seconds? If I do think about it a little bit more, this silly example can serve as a guide to my behavior in daily life.

48 COMMITMENT
Leaving Iraq

My most recent return from Iraq marked a bittersweet homecoming. I'd written PowerfulPeace.net from the mixed-up belly of war for more than a year. Odd as it may sound, leaving war and returning to the comforts of home and loved ones bring strange, uncomfortable feelings to a guy like me. If you've also been blessed to return from war, you understand.

Instead of expecting to restrain forever the capacity to wage war, you've got to change the attitude of people who control...war-making machines and who make the decision to use them.
J. William Fulbright

With a few more weeks or days at war, my advice might have still inspired a commander to take a slightly different course; that change might have resulted in one American life saved or one Iraqi child unharmed by a terrorist attack. In the States, I don't feel such immediate influence on the fight—the potential loss weighs heavy. To bring just one more young husband home would be worth the cost of my entire career. I suspect you would feel the same, if you think about it.

I left good friends who would carry on in the effort for peace and stability for months to follow. As a consultant, I choose when and where I go. As Service members, they go when and where Uncle Sam so dictates. They continued (and continue) to strive there long past my return to the land of Starbucks.

That attack had only a handful of rockets, but
the one closest to me killed a man...again.

Back in "the world," I go about business as usual, see friends and family regularly, and get pretty regular sleep. I don't need to throw myself into the dust by the side of the road because IDF (indirect fire) has exploded a hundred yards from me, as happened in that final week...again.

That attack had only a handful of rockets, but the one closest to me killed a man...again.

In war, I can look into the eyes of the leader who must manage a plan for and respond to such attacks. I can recommend variations to complement our violent action and hear the commander say, "I never thought about it that way." I can see results unfold over time as conditions ease for the citizenry and worsen for the enemy. That corresponds to a reduction of threat to both our forces and innocent civilians.

Back in the world, I don't have my eyes, hands and ideas on the problem set so well. I lose the ground truth insight that comes from being, well, on the ground. The palpable hates, hopes and hungers that saturate the very air of Iraq are missing back in Washington. We imagine we grasp what's going on 6,000 miles away—we don't. It's comfortable, back home, and I think these wars take on a status akin to scenery for the real show in America: the economy.

Several of my friends were killed in the 2005 Op Redwing in Afghanistan. I encourage you to read about it in Marcus Luttrell's book, *Lone Survivor: The Eyewitness Account of Operation Redwing and the Lost Heroes of SEAL Team 10* (Little, Brown and Company, 2007). Although this tragedy occurred before my Navy retirement, I had already begun my antiterrorism work in DC, away from the SEAL Teams, and I heard about it on the news like everybody else. Unlike everybody else, these were guys with whom I had fought, trained, and laughed. The deeply painful sense that

...these were guys with whom I had fought,
trained, and laughed. The deeply painful sense
that I had abandoned them was intense...

There is no "done" for those who are built to serve, at least not until breath itself is done.

I had abandoned them was intense, as was the irrational conviction that "if only" I had been with that special reconnaissance squad on that mission on that day, things might have turned out differently. I do know better, but it doesn't reduce the sense of guilt. Marcus and I have talked about this at length. I dedicated my retirement ceremony to Dan Healy with the words of Proverbs 27:17, "As iron sharpens iron, so one man sharpens another." We used to have some great fights on the mats.

Leaving comrades is a difficult thing, even if the destination is delightful. Every veteran has experienced it. Home calls to you; the thought of family and picnics and safety pulls at you…yet looking at those who stay behind makes you reluctant to go. Remember Charlie Sheen's character flying away at the end of *Platoon* (MGM, 1986), smiling sadly back at his brothers on the ground. In the war.

Just Google our combat wounded to hear their stories. The most common refrain, even from the amputees, is "Please send me back in, Sir. My boys need me!"

The duty to one's comrades, developed through shared urgency, is strong. I will never stop trying to make a difference for those in need. There is no "done" for those who are built to serve, at least not until breath itself is done. I'll strive in DC, back in Iraq and around the world to share and expand these ideas. I believe you will carry some of them, too, and recognize and write some of your own. I look forward to hearing from you—and working with you—on *our* next project for balanced peacemaking. You'll read more about how to do that in the Conclusion. We can commit together to continuous awareness and the endless search for peace opportunities. We can devote the strength of our Bodies to making this a way of life. We can exert out Minds to greater creativity, and open our Hearts. We can listen to the guidance from our Souls. We can strive to all be comrades…in Powerful Peace.

So that's it. Parting is, in fact, such sweet sorrow.

Goodbye, Iraq.

…I'll see you soon.

INTO ACTION PLAN IV

- Read Schwartz, *The Magic of Thinking Big*
- Read USIP's *Women and War*
- Read Flynn, Pottinger and Batchelor, *"Fixing Intelligence"*
- Read Luttrell, *Lone Survivor: The Eyewitness Account of Operation Redwing and the Lost Heroes of SEAL Team 10*
- Watch *Platoon*
- Read Christakis and Fowler, *Connected; How Your Friends' Friends' Friends Affect Everything you Feel, Think, and Do*

CONCLUSION
Hope

In the end, we find ourselves in the beginning. The brief introduction that is this book is only the first taste of the potential of Powerful Peace. If and how balanced peacemaking continues is up to you and me, together. Powerful Peace will grow through reading, and sharing, and doing…or it will not grow at all.

> **I want you to consider making**
> **your life one long gift to others….**
> **All that lasts is what you pass on.**
> **The rest is smoke and mirrors.**
> *Stephen King*

I promised you up front that we would examine the "reactive and sometimes unnecessary roots of hate," and that you would come to better understand how "those roots strangle all involved." Have we done that? I hope so. I hope at least one or two of the dozens of stories in Powerful Peace have helped you look at conflict differently. Most bonfires begin with a tiny spark, so let us let peace "go viral." And the highest praise I've ever heard on these concepts came from my editor's wife, Virginia, when she first told him, "I never thought of it that way before."

We've also explored the paradox of "necessary violence" with "ruthless restraint," and the principle that balancing courage with compassion applies in the boardroom, in the bedroom, and on the battlefield. I'd like to wind down this book with a

This is Allem, a contract cleaner from Bangladesh. He took great care of us in Iraq. Allem doesn't chase after glory and excitement, yet he's a real hero in my eyes because he takes good care of his family. (Pay no mind to the bandage on my brow— it was from a tragic soccer accident.)

last word, one of my favorites, which you may have noticed tucked here and there throughout the chapters: Hope.

One of my many friends from the wider world is a highly-placed officer in the Iraqi Army. Khudaier and I sometimes chatted over fruit juice on the way ahead in Iraq. Like many of his peers, he has invaluable insight on problems and solutions regarding the struggle. Also like many of his peers, his recommendations (the other-than-combat efforts we all need for a long-term "win") sometimes compete with more immediate U.S./Western needs for force protection and combat readiness. Yet he and I contend that this apparent "competition" between national and international resources and goals is not as real as is imagined…or rather, is *not* imagined. I contend that "our" way ahead as a species depends less on struggling over crusts and more on exercising all our imagination muscles to make more pie.

He insisted, and I agreed, that more trust between our forces was urgently needed to improve our effectiveness. Yet hope, we concluded, is the most urgent commodity we can offer to the men and women of that ancient, noble and profoundly historic land. There are many other essential ingredients as described throughout Powerful Peace; most of them are merely steps along the path to hope.

Another friend, Jamal, lost his family home, lifelong friends and fiancée when he was identified as an American supporter. He also lost hope, although when I first

---

…"our" way ahead as a species depends less on struggling over crusts and more on exercising all our imagination muscles to make more pie.

met him, his confidence was unshakeable. Barely out of his teens, Jamal had left a university computer science program and hired on to interpret Arabic for U.S. forces. I asked him why he had been willing to leave the sure thing of school to enter the dangerous world of military operations. He said he had a vision for his country. He had a beautiful girlfriend, and they were in love. She would become his wife once he had enough money. And once "we" (Coalition and Iraqis) inevitably stabilized the internal strife, his country would need strong, intelligent people to step forward and lead it to prosperity. Wise beyond his years, he understood that those who were in the proper positions when stability arrived would be well-placed to assume those leadership roles. He would become a Big Man and make a difference for the people of his nation.

Jamal and other interpreters were sometimes unnecessarily kept waiting outside the ECP guard shack for several hours while their credentials were "verified" by U.S. soldiers, some of whom were literally still in their teens. (These interpreters all carried official photo identification cards, but "slow rolling" a customer is the questionable indulgence of petty tyrants the world over.) During the same assignment I met weekly with another Iraqi general officer who repeatedly expressed frustration that "your men are disrespecting my officers." Jamal's was not an isolated case.

(You have to understand that I'm not indicting all American soldiers here. American soldiers are Americans, like me, and I'm damn proud of my country and my countrymen. I also understand that we're not perfect. Sadly, the kids who helped this unfortunate situation go badly probably only did what they'd been taught by older soldiers…who had learned from others before that. And the problem of disrespect to foreigners is by no means limited to U.S. forces. I've personally been disrespected by some of the best; in Russia, Thailand, Kuwait and a couple dozen other nations. But remember—we can only change what we control, and we only control ourselves.)

During the time Jamal and I were at that installation, local insurgents would periodically cruise by with the traffic to scope out the gates; on one of these passes,

---

During the same assignment I met weekly with another Iraqi general officer who repeatedly expressed frustration that "your men are disrespecting my officers."

Jamal had lost hope through a radically narrowed range of possibilities for his future, but I believe hope can be restored as long as we draw breath.

---

inevitably, one of the neighbor boys recognized Jamal as he sat outside the entrance for hours. Word got back to the insurgents in the neighborhood. His father received an anonymous phone call that their home would be firebombed to kill Jamal's younger siblings. The father fled with his family.

Jamal's future father-in-law heard next, and declared that his daughter would never marry a traitorous "pig" who worked for the invaders. Jamal's own childhood friends shunned him on his final visit home, so he only learned of his imminent danger through a remote grapevine.

It saddens me almost to tears to remember that promising young man, with such incredible talent, hope and energy; and the hopeless, vacant young man who returned to our base after that weekend. In our final conversation before I moved to another location in Iraq, I half-jokingly asked my friend, "You're not going to become an insurgent, are you?"

He paused, then said quietly, "I don't know."

This was a preventable disaster in one young person's life. Not all can be avoided, of course. Automobiles and airplanes will continue to crash. Disease will continue to strike. But if I can get across only one idea through all of this, it would be that we can easily harm others through minor, selfish choices. A little thought goes a long way, even if it's only to reduce potential backlash against ourselves.

Jamal had lost hope through a radically narrowed range of possibilities for his future, but I believe hope can be restored as long as we draw breath. Our species has survived plague, famine, barbarian hordes, Crusades, and World Wars. I imagine it has sometimes been difficult to hold onto hope. Yet it survives, and it can be revived, for some of the hundreds, thousands, and millions of decent people who can't take their children to the market with them for fear of car bombs...or simply can't feed their children because they can't afford food. At the purely individual level, I want women who feel hopelessly trapped in abusive relationships to rediscover hope, as well as young people who feel too fat or too skinny to be of any worth. The same goes for men of the "wrong" race or class in societies that traditionally suppress their opportunities. In my own selfish way, I want human beings to be valued universally.

In my own selfish way, I want human beings to be valued universally. I'm telling you now: this will bring a corresponding element of security.

I'm telling you now: this will bring a corresponding element of security. The world has changed in many, many ways. Shame on us if we don't keep up with history, look at one another in the best light possible, and invite the best from all. Each individual's increase benefits the whole. Shame on us if we participate in reducing ourselves.

Hope is something that can be given, although it can never be forced. A person cannot be "convinced" of something against his will. Hope can be *inspired*, by example, as when the United States of America still inspires the hope of a better life for millions who live in tragic poverty or lawlessness. Hope can be *revealed*, in the genuine, consistent effort of outreach from those who have it to those who don't. Once we grasp hope firmly in our hands, we begin to perceive the extraordinary future we can create.

The energy of hope can produce startling results. In the book *Let's Roll* (Tyndale House Publishers, 2002), we read of true heroes, doomed passengers on a hijacked aircraft on September 11, 2001. They knew something very bad was going to happen with their plane. They realized there might not be anything they could do about it… but they hoped they could. They hoped they could, and they acted.

These heroes saw no gain in hiding amid the herd and praying not to be the next one culled. They dared to act in the hope of stopping terrorists with their own hands. They succeeded. Powered by this hope, they saved hundreds or thousands of other innocent lives. They died, yes—they successfully stopped terrorists and they still died, because fighting to defend involves daring and risk; some always pay the price for the rest.

Will you dare to hope with me? Will you dare to question your assumptions about people in the next house, or on the next continent? I also said in the front of

Each individual's increase benefits the whole. Shame on us if we participate in reducing ourselves.

the book that it's intended to offer a voice to all, to open a dialogue. That dialogue begins at PeaceHawks.org. You get your voice there, whether you're sitting in Baghdad, Paris, Capetown or with me in Washington, DC. Through the site, you can submit your own ideas to our blog at PowerfulPeace.net. As a Peace Hawk, you'll learn about and join with organizations like the Middle East Peace project at MEPeace.org, where Eyal Raviv and our friends host an ongoing dialogue among all the stakeholders of the Israel-Palestine crisis. Engagement matters. They prove it in real time. We engaged citizens will no longer sit by and wait for heads of state to solve all the problems within or between our societies. Here's a dirty little secret: they can't.

As a Peace Hawk, you'll also be able to link to the "Enough Project" of John Prendergast and Don Cheadle, at EnoughMoment.org. Click in to look around at the stories from film superstars as well as compassion superstars – see where *you* can make a difference!

Hope is our energy; imagination and action are our tools. Let these closing words be the opening salvo on your lifelong contribution to practical peace—step away from the sofa and call up a friend to offer some heartfelt Dignity and Respect, or reflect on what sections of Powerful Peace struck you most…and what it is inside you that may have motivated this response. You might even start your own reading group, or a local chapter of Peace Hawks, to spread the ideas in your community. There are 48 topical chapters in the book, not counting this one on Hope. How would you like to organize a study of one topic each week throughout the year with your church, mosque, temple or coffee clutch?

Before his private world imploded, Jamal made one other comment that will stay with me forever: "If more Americans thought like you, there'd be less wars in the world." Well, I doubt I'll actually ever prevent a war, but I do believe the concepts of Powerful Peace can empower each of us to reduce conflict within the scope of our own authority and influence. Of course this goes for my American friends, with our substantial international impact, and also to my Afghan, British, Canadian, French, Iraqi, Jordanian, Kenyan, Russian, Uzbek, Venezuelan and other friends as well.

Jamal made one other comment that will stay with me forever: "If more Americans thought like you, there'd be less wars in the world."

Together we have the power to make a difference. Say it with me: we have the power to make a difference. This is the start of something big.

Finally: in the beginning, I asked that you "not keep this book." I asked you to "give it away—perhaps to a young person just setting out to make a mark in the world, or to your neighbor, or to a soldier trying to make sense of his painful experiences...perhaps to your senator at her next public event."

I really mean that. If these ideas make sense to you, will you share them with others? They say selling a book is much more about word-of-mouth than about formal advertising; I say selling an *idea* is even more dependent on each one reaching one. If every reader shared this book just one time, it would double the spread of this message around the world. It will take willing and active individuals to make meaningful change and protect all our children. I promise you, I'll keep trying. Will you accept the challenge and do the same?

I dare you to.

ABOUT THE AUTHOR

J. Robert DuBois is a security and policy advisor who was labeled a "smart power authority" while assisting U.S., British and Iraqi forces in Baghdad. A multilingual Navy SEAL with professional experience in more than thirty countries, he retired from military service in 2006...then headed back to Iraq and Afghanistan in support of commanders struggling with complex threat situations. Rob has presented his "Think like the Adversary" workshop to military units in the hottest combat zones, Fortune 500 corporate customers, and government organizations from the National Counterterrorism Center to the Fort Knox Mint Police. He has served on the Deputy Secretary of Defense's Senior Integration Group (SIG), led the DoD's Red Team operations, and is Chairman of the National Security Subcommittee of the Homeland Security Foundation of America. Rob is also Chief Security Officer for the AllHumanity Group, which works to ensure dependable, *accountable* delivery of humanitarian resources and services to crisis areas worldwide. Founder and CEO of VoDuBo Consulting, Rob lives with his family in the Washington, DC area and works anywhere on the planet. For questions, comments or appearances, please write Robert@PowerfulPeace.net.

LIST OF TERMS AND ABBREVIATIONS

AQ	al Qaeda
AQI	al Qaeda in Iraq
ASP	Applied Smart Power
AT	Antiterrorism
C2	Command and Control
CA	Civil Affairs
CAP	Cause a Pause
CT	Counterterrorism
DFAC	Dining Facility
DoD	Department of Defense
DoS	Department of State
ECP	Entry Control Point ("base gate")
HAL	Human Aspect of Life
IED	Improvised Explosive Device ("roadside bomb")
IDF	Indirect Fire (rockets and mortars)
IO	Information Operations
KKK	Ku Klux Klan
MRE	Meal, Ready-to-eat
NAF	New America Foundation
OBL	Osama bin Laden
OMEH	Overwhelming Middle Eastern Hospitality
OPSEC	Operational Security
ORH	Overwhelming Russian Hospitality
PBIED	Personnel-borne Improvised Explosive Device ("suicide bomber")
R&R	Rest and Recuperation
RAT	Reachable and Teachable
RPG	Rocket Propelled Grenade

SDV   SEAL Delivery Vehicle (Navy SEAL free-flooding minisubmarine, which I sometimes piloted during my Team years)

SEAL   The acronym designating Navy commandos was taken from the environments in which they would be prepared to operate: "Sea, Air, and Land"

SIG   Senior Integration Group

SOCOM Special Operations Command

SR   Special Reconnaissance (my primary mission set while in the Teams)

Trident   Navy SEAL insignia pin (also known as the "Budweiser," or "chicken on a fork")

UDT   Underwater Demolition Team (predecessor to the Navy SEAL Teams)

USIP   United States Institute of Peace

VA   Veterans' Administration

VBIED   Vehicle-borne Improvised Explosive Device ("car bomb," but specifically designates a car bomb that's moving, or "-borne")

RESOURCES

As with any avid reader and concerned citizen, I've been influenced by many sources across many fields. Below are some of my favorites. I invite you to browse through the titles and see what catches your eye. Each offers valuable insights.

Top ten recommendations for increasing context (alpha by author):

Terrorists in Love; The Real Lives of Islamic Radicals (Free Press, 2011) **Ballen**

The Interrogator; An Education (Nation Books, 2011) **Carle**

Shake Hands with the Devil; The Failure of Humanity in Rwanda (Da Capo Press, 2003) **Dallaire**

The Tipping Point; How Little Things Can Make a Big Difference (Little, Brown and Co., 2000) **Gladwell**

The Heart and The Fist: The Education of a Humanitarian, the Making of a Navy SEAL (Houghton Mifflin Harcourt, 2011) **Greitens**

The Radical Center; The Future of American Politics (Anchor Books, 2001) **Halstead and Lind**

The Islamist; Why I Became an Islamic Fundamentalist, What I Saw Inside, and Why I left (Penguin Books, 2007) **Husain**

How to Run the World; Charting a Course to the Next Renaissance (Random House, 2011) **Khanna**

Blackwater; The Rise of the World's Most Powerful Mercenary Army (Nation Books, 2007) **Scahill**

Sacred Rage; The Wrath of Militant Islam (Touchstone, 2001) **Wright**

Recommended reading list (not already referenced in text, alpha by author):

The 9/11 Commission Report; Final Report of the National Commission on Terrorist Attacks upon the United States (W. W. Norton and Co., 2004) **The 9/11 Commission**

The Lessons of Terror; A History of Warfare Against Civilians (Random House, 2003) **Carr**

One Perfect Op; An Insider's Account of the Navy SEAL Special Warfare Teams (HarperCollins, 2002) **Chalker**

Tribes; We Need YOU to Lead Us (Penguin Books, 2008) **Godin**

On Killing; The Psychological Cost of Learning to Kill in War and Society (Little, Brown and Co., 1995) **Grossman**

The Most Dangerous Place; Pakistan's Lawless Frontier (Viking, 2009) **Gul**

Inside Terrorism (Columbia University Press, 1998) **Hoffman**

The Iraq Study Group Report; A Way Forward—A New Approach (Vintage, 2006) **The Iraq Study Group**

The 80/20 Principle; The Secret to Achieving More with Less (Doubleday, 1998) **Koch**

Meditations on Violence; A Comparison of Martial Arts Training and Real World Violence (YMAA Publishing Center, 2008) **Miller**

A National Party no More; The Conscience of a Conservative Democrat (Stroud and Hall, 2003) **Miller**

Understanding Arabs; A Guide for Westerners (Intercultural Press, 1996) **Nydell**

Inside the Wire; A Military Intelligence Soldier's Eyewitness Account of Life at Guantanamo (The Penguin Press, 2005) **Saar and Novak**

Facing Down Evil; Life on the Edge as an FBI Hostage Negotiator (G. P. Putnam's Sons, 2006) **Van Zandt**

Books referenced and recommended in the text (alpha by author):

Getting Things Done; The Art of Stress-Free Productivity (Penguin Books, 2001) **Allen**

Making It All Work; Winning at the Game of Work and Business of Life (Viking Adult, 2008) **Allen**

Beyond Fundamentalism; Confronting Religious Extremism in the Age of Globalization (Random House, 2009) **Aslan**

Fixing Intel; A Blueprint for Making Intelligence Relevant in Afghanistan (CNAS, 2010) **Batchelor, Flynn and Pottinger**

Holy War, Inc.; Inside the Secret World of Osama bin Laden (Touchstone, 2001) **Bergen**

The Longest War: The Enduring Conflict between America and al-Qaeda (Free
    Press, 2011) **Bergen**

The Osama bin Laden I Know (Free Press, 2006) **Bergen**

7 Habits of Highly Effective People (Free Press, 1990) **Covey**

Principle-Centered Leadership (Fireside, 1992) **Covey**

*Connected; How Your Friends' Friends' Friends Affect Everything you Feel, Think,
    and Do* (Little, Brown and Company, 2009) **Christakis and Fowler**

Invisible History; Afghanistan's Untold Story (City Lights Publishers, 2009)
    Fitzgerald and Gould

Half the Sky; Turning Oppression into Opportunity for Women Worldwide (Alfred
    A. Knopf, 2009) **Kristof and WuDunn**

*Lone Survivor: The Eyewitness Account of Operation Redwing and the Lost Heroes
    of SEAL Team 10* (Little, Brown and Company, 2007) **Luttrell**

Ultimate Jujutsu: Principles and Practice (Strider Nolan Publishing, 2002)
    Maberry

CSIS Commission on Smart Power; A smarter, more secure America (Center for
    Strategic and International Studies, 2007) **Nye and Armitage**

The Future of Power (PublicAffairs, 2011) **Nye**

Soft Power; The Means to Success in World Politics (PublicAffairs, 2004) **Nye**

The Enough Moment (Three Rivers Press, 2010) **Prendergast**

The Magic of Thinking Big (Fireside, 1959) **Schwartz**

Women and War (Endowment of the United States Institute of Peace, 2011)
    United States Institute of Peace

A Spy's Resume; Confessions of a Maverick *Intelligence Professional and*
    Misadventure *Capitalist* (Scarecrow Press, 2008) **Viola**

*World at Risk; The Report of the Commission on the Prevention of Weapons of
    Mass Destruction Proliferation and Terrorism* (Vintage Books, 2008)
    WMD Commission

Moment of Truth in Iraq (Richard Vigilante, 2008) Yon

Films mentioned in Powerful Peace (alpha by title):

Blackhawk Down (Revolution Studios, 2001)

Crash (Lion's Gate, 2004)

Full Metal Jacket (Warner Bros., 1987)

Hotel Rwanda (MGM/United Artists, 2004)

John Q (New Line Cinema, 2002)

Liar, Liar (Universal, 1997)

The Naked Gun (Paramount Pictures, 1988)

Reno 911 (Series, Comedy Central)

The Russians are Coming, the Russians are Coming! (United Artists, 1966)

Platoon (MGM, 1986)